500

pizzas & flatbreads

500

pizzas & flatbreads

Rebecca Baugniet

APPLE

A Quintet Book

First published in the UK in 2008 by
Apple Press
7 Greenland Street
London NW1 0ND
United Kingdom

www.apple-press.com

ISBN: 978-1-84543-270-6
QTT.PZB

This book was conceived, designed, and produced by
Quintet Publishing Limited
6 Blundell Street
London N7 9BH
United Kingdom

Project Editor: Marianne Canty
Designer: Roland Codd
Art Director: Sofia Henry
Photographer: Mike McClafferty
Food Stylist: Wendy Lee
Managing Editor: Donna Gregory
Publisher: James Tavendale

10 9 8 7 6 5 4 3 2 1

Manufactured in Singapore by Pica Digital Pte Ltd.
Printed in China by SNP Leefung Printers Ltd.

contents

introduction	6
pizza basics	14
pan pizzas	30
thin crust pizzas	58
rustic pizzas & calzones	86
international pizzas	114
fougasse, foccacia & european flatbreads	142
indian & african flatbreads	170
flatbreads & hearth breads of the middle east	198
flatbreads of the americas	222
sweet pizzas and flatbreads	252
index	282

introduction

Flatbread has existed for as long as humans have been grinding grains, mixing the resulting flour with water, and baking over hot coals. And for almost just as long, people have made these flatbreads more interesting by covering them with other assorted ingredients.

It is the oldest variety of prepared food – one that appears all over the globe, but that takes on different shapes and textures from region to region, depending on which basic ingredients are available in that part of the world. Ancient Greeks called theirs "plakuntos" and covered them with blends of herbs, garlic, and onion. The Aztecs called theirs "tlaxcalli" and made them with maize, which had first been soaked in water mixed with lime to help remove the husks and soften the grain. Many flatbread recipes have survived through the ages and remain close to those original culinary discoveries. They feature flours made from one or more grains – wheat, millet, rye, maize, rice, and buckwheat, to name but a few. They may also be made from grated tubers or root vegetables, such as potatoes, cassava, beetroots and turnips. With the advent of the global food market, those living in urban areas and even those removed from the city – with access to the Internet and home delivery – can taste flavours from far-off countries and evoke memories of ancient civilizations in their own home kitchens.

Flatbreads fall into two main categories – those leavened with yeast or another leavening agent, and those that are unleavened. In the category of leavened flatbread, pizza is the one that has become a truly international phenomenon over the past 60 years, although focaccias, pittas, naans, and others have been gaining more widespread popularity. What sets pizza apart from other flatbreads is the use of tomato as the main topping ingredient. This became common practice around Naples in the eighteenth century and rapidly grew in fame throughout Italy. One hundred years later, pizza was brought to the United States by Italian immigrants and began another metamorphosis. Pizzerias began appearing in cities throughout the country and soon different trends in pizza-making started to emerge, with such delicious results as the Chicago deep-dish pizza, thin base pizzas and pan pizzas.

In response to these developments, Neapolitan pizza makers formed an association in 1984 to protect the characteristics of the original Neapolitan pizza, imposing specific rules to be obeyed in order for a pizza to qualify as authentically Neapolitan. The association accepts only Marinara and Margherita Pizzas made entirely by hand – no mixers or rolling pins allowed. They must measure no more than 30 cm (12 in) across and be baked in a wood-fired oven for no more than a minute and a half. Fortunately, the "True Neapolitan Pizza Association" will not be inspecting your kitchen, so have fun and experiment with your favorite topping combinations. Whichever recipe you try first, when you take part in this time-honored process, you are sure to enjoy the results.

equipment

If you plan on making pizzas and flatbreads on a regular basis, you may want to invest in a few pieces of equipment that will encourage successful results, such as a baking stone and a pizza peel. However, these items are not essential to the process, and most of the recipes in this book can be made with ordinary kitchen items.

measuring cups & spoons
Baking is an exact science, so correct measuring equipment is essential. Always weigh ingredients carefully, using accurate scales, and measure liquids in a calibrated measuring jug. Flour should be spooned into measuring cups for accurate measurements.

mixing bowls & standing mixers
A variety of mixing bowls is essential in the baker's kitchen. You will need a large bowl in which to make the dough and let it rise. A glass 2-litre (3½ pint) measuring bowl can be especially useful for measuring how much your dough has risen. Medium and small bowls are useful for preparing fillings and toppings. A standing mixer with a dough hook attachment allows you to perform other tasks in the kitchen while the dough is being kneaded.

rolling pins & boards
Pizza purists will insist that pizza dough must be stretched out by hand, but until you have mastered this technique, a rolling pin is a very useful tool. Many models of rolling pin are available, so choose one that suits your needs and which you find comfortable to work with. The preferred model among bakers remains the wooden French rolling pin with tapered ends. However, in a pinch, you can always use an empty wine bottle. A large wooden board is ideal for rolling out pizza dough, but a well-cleaned worktop will also work nicely.

pizza peels, baking stones & tiles

A pizza peel, or paddle, is a flat, smooth, rounded board with a long handle and tapered front edge that facilitates sliding the pizza on and off the baking stone or tiles. It is usually made of hardwood, but it can also be found in aluminium. A flat baking sheet can also be used as a makeshift pizza peel. Baking stones or quarry tiles are used for making pizzas and flatbreads that require a direct burst of heat to achieve a crisp base, such as thin-base pizzas, pizza with a Neapolitan base, and flatbreads such as naan and pitta (which are traditionally baked on oven floors or walls). Baking stones are thick, heavy, round or rectangular pieces of natural lead-free clay that mimic the baking conditions of brick-floored wood-burning ovens. Baking stones are placed on the bottom rack of electric ovens and directly on the floor of a gas oven and preheated with the oven. Unglazed quarry tiles may also be used for the same effect. Peels and baking stones are available in various sizes from gourmet specialty stores or online kitchen equipment suppliers.

frying pans, baking pans, baking sheets & baking paper

Heavy 23-cm (9-in) cast-iron frying pans can be used for baking pan pizzas, as can 23-cm (9-in) cake pans or a large rimmed rectangular baking sheet. Chicago-style deep-dish pizzas can be made in 23-cm (9-in) round cake pans; however, specialty deep-dish pizza pans are available in different sizes from online distributors. Baking paper is good for lining baking pans, and it is also useful if you are having trouble transferring your pizza dough from the peel to the baking stone. Simply roll the pizza dough directly onto a square of baking paper for easy transfers.

tortilla & chapatti presses; tavas & warmers

Specialty equipment is available for certain flatbreads, such as tortillas. If you are making a large quantity of tortillas, you may wish to invest in a tortilla press. These are available in aluminum, cast-iron, plastic and wood. There's even an electric model that presses and bakes the tortilla in one step. Similar to the tortilla press is the chapatti press, made of cast-iron with two stainless steel plates inside. Tavas are the flat, rimless metal frying pans used for frying chapattis and rotis. These can also be used for making tortillas and other flatbreads. Neither the tortilla press nor the chapatti press is essential to making these flatbreads, but they do help speed up the process if you're making them in large quantities. If you have a good, flat frying pan or griddle, you can use it for a variety of flatbreads. Tortilla warmers are available in terracotta, porcelain, silicone and as woven baskets. They can be used to keep tortillas and other flatbreads warm throughout the meal.

timers

When baking pizzas and flatbreads, timing is crucial. Either use the timer on your oven or invest in an inexpensive, accurate digital timer.

ingredients

While the dough for pizzas and flatbreads requires only a few ingredients — flour, yeast, salt, olive oil, and water — the toppings can be as plain or as exotic, mild, or aromatic as you choose. Try to use the freshest ingredients whenever possible. Organic ingredients that have been produced free of any chemicals or pesticides will always result in the tastiest baked goods.

wheat & other grain flours

Most recipes for the pizzas in this book call for a blend of plain flour and bread flour. Bread flour contains slightly more gluten than plain flour and helps give the base its crispy quality.

Experiment with different blends of flour to find the perfect base for your tastes. Wholemeal flour can replace a portion of the plain flour, but it will result in a somewhat rougher texture. Masa harina is the ideal ingredient for making corn tortillas, though fine cornmeal can be used. Certain flatbread recipes in this book call for flours made from other grains, such as barley, buckwheat, rye, and teff. These are becoming easier to find in the organic sections of larger grocery stores, as well as in health food stores.

yeast & other leavening agents

Yeast is a microscopic single-cell organism commonly used as a leavening agent in breads. Baker's yeast is available as traditional active dried yeast, easy-blend dried yeast, and compressed fresh yeast. Easy-blend dried yeast, as the name implies, shortens the time it takes to leaven the dough, but is sometimes criticized by bakers who believe that bread and pizza dough requires a longer rising time to achieve the best flavour and texture. Fresh compressed yeast must be refrigerated and used within two weeks. A basic rule for yeast substitutions is 1x 7 g ($^1/_4$ oz) sachet of active dried yeast equals 10 ml (2 tsp) of easy-blend dried yeast or 1 cake of compressed yeast. To "proof" yeast, or test whether it is still alive, dissolve it in warm water, adding a pinch of sugar, and set aside 5 to 10 minutes. If it begins to swell and foam, then it is alive and will act as a leavening agent. Baking powder and bicarbonate of soda are used as leavening agents in some flatbreads and are commonly available in supermarkets.

oil

Extra-virgin olive oil is used in all recipes unless otherwise specified. Italians add crushed red pepper flakes to olive oil to make "olio santo", which is drizzled in a clockwise motion over a pizza fresh out of the oven.

water

High levels of chlorine and some minerals found in some tap water can have an impact on the action of the yeast in dough. If you are having difficulty with yeast that you are sure is viable, switch to bottled or purified water. In the recipes "warm" water indicates water between 40 to 46°C (105°F–115°F). Water that is too cold will not activate yeast, while water that is too hot will kill it. "Tepid" water refers to water at room temperature.

herbs, spices & seeds

Fresh herbs will guarantee the most flavourful sauces and toppings, but dried herbs are an acceptable substitute. A basic rule for herb substitutions is 5 g (1 tsp) chopped fresh herbs equals 1.25 g ($\frac{1}{4}$ tsp) of dried and crumbled herbs. Italian herbs such as basil, oregano, and flat-leaf parsley, are all frequently used in pizzas and calzones, so you will want to have them on hand. A wide variety of spices and seeds are used in flatbreads – sesame, poppy, caraway, and flax seeds, which are all widely available in grocery shops. Check health food stores and speciality spice shops for more obscure seeds.

tomatoes & vegetables

Tomatoes grown in the San Marzano region of Italy are the variety preferred by most pizza makers. If buying canned tomatoes, check the labels to make sure they are indeed a product of Italy. If they are not available in your area, try out different brands of canned tomatoes to find the ones with the best flavour. Use canned whole tomatoes, as seeds that have been crushed during processing add bitterness to the flavour. If you are using canned hopped tomatoes, you may want to add a bit of sugar to reduce bitterness. Start with 1.25 g ($\frac{1}{4}$ tsp) sugar and add more to taste. If making sauce from fresh tomatoes, opt for vine-ripened ones with a good, strong tomato aroma. Always use the freshest produce you can find. Patronizing local farmers for seasonal produce will guarantee the best flavour as well as being environmentally responsible.

cheeses, sausage & cured meats

Pizzas are the ultimate showcases for all the best Italian cheeses. If you live near a good cheese store, you will have no trouble acquiring authentic mozzarella, ricotta, Parmesan, Asiago, Taleggio, fontina, and provolone. Otherwise, online distributors usually offer overnight delivery. The recipes in this book call for shredded mozzarella – this refers to the block mozzarella available in supermarkets and made popular on American pan pizzas. Fresh mozzarella is the more authentic Italian cheese of choice; it is referred to as bocconcini. It should be used in slices or in torn pieces. Small balls of fresh mozzarella are referred to as bocconcini. Do not limit yourself to Italian cheeses, however, as other cheeses also make luscious toppings for pizzas and flatbread. Chèvre (goat's cheese), Boursin, St. Agur, and Gorgonzola are all used with spectacular results in this book. Sausage, removed from its casings and crumbled, is often used as a topping or in sauces. Use a fresh sausage such as an Italian sausage, or one that better suits your tastes. Cured meats such as pancetta, prosciutto, mortadella, and salami are all widely available at supermarket deli counters or Italian deli shops.

store-bought pizza dough & bases

When you crave pizza but haven't got the time to make your own dough, shop-bought pizza dough is a fine alternative. Good-quality prepared pizza dough is on sale both frozen and pre-cooked. Find one that best suits your tastes, or try out other pre-made flatbreads, such as pitta or naan, as a base for your homemade pizza. English muffins are the perfect size for children's mini pizzas – top with pizza sauce and some grated cheese and pop under a hot grill until the cheese has melted for an almost-instant snack.

pizza basics

making pizzas & flatbreads

While any kind of bread-making may have the reputation of being too time-consuming or difficult, once you have succeeded in producing a beautiful pizza or flatbread you will see what a misconception this is. Most pizza and flatbread recipes are easily divided into a series of small tasks, each one taking no more than a few minutes. Choose a recipe according to your needs. If you are in a hurry, you may wish to skip some steps by using shop-bought pizza base, pizza sauce, and pre-grated mozzarella.

If you want to make your pizza dough ahead of time, it can be placed in the refrigerator to rise, as the cool temperature slows the rising process. Place the divided portions of dough in individual large sealable bags, pressing down the dough to flatten it into a disc and removing the air from the bags. Repeat this three times, at one-hour intervals. The dough can then be left in the refrigerator for up to 24 hours. When you want to use the dough, let it reach room temperature and rise for an additional 2 to 3 hours.

If you are making the dough the day you plan to make your pizzas, be sure to leave enough time for the dough to rise. This time can vary from 10 minutes to 2 to 3 hours depending on the dough you are making. Yeasted dough should be covered lightly and placed in a warm, draught-free place to rise. If you live in a cold climate and your kitchen is cool and draughty, turn on your oven to 180°C (350°F / Gas Mark 4) as you begin preparing the dough.

Let the oven heat up for 5 minutes, and then turn it off completely. Once you have prepared the dough, place it in the oven to rise, checking that the oven is just warm and not actually hot enough to bake your dough.

When rolling out dough, let it rest for a few minutes after you have rolled it once. Allow dough to relax into its new shape for 1 to 2 minutes, then continue rolling.

preparing to bake

Make sure to read through the recipe well before you plan to bake, to establish how long you will need to get from start to finish as well as to verify that you have all the necessary ingredients on hand. Baking involves using many kitchen surfaces for all the various steps, so it is always a good idea to start with a clean kitchen.

Once you have read through the recipe and have all the ingredients on hand, you are ready to start! The oven temperatures in recipes are listed before placing the pizza or flatbread in the oven, but to achieve the classic crispy-based base, you need to have a very hot preheated oven and baking stone. Place the baking stone or tiles in the oven, to preheat for an hour. Use the hottest temperature on your oven, which will generally be 240°C (475°F, Gas Mark 9). If your oven is capable of a higher temperature, use that but keep a close eye on your pizza to prevent burning. If you are uncertain about your oven's accuracy, use an oven thermometer, sold in hardware kitchen shops. If you find your pizza base is burning on the bottom before the top has cooked, reduce the oven temperature by 5-10°C (25-50°F) or raise the baking stone by one level.

Prepare your sauce and all the toppings while the dough is rising, and work quickly once your pizza base has been placed on the peel. Gently shake your pizza peel to make sure the dough is not sticking and will transfer easily to the stone. Add a little flour or cornmeal to the peel to prevent sticking, or place a sheet of baking paper on the peel under the base. Pizzas and flatbreads bake quickly on a hot baking stone, so stay in the kitchen and keep an eye on how it is doing for your first few attempts. You may need to adjust the oven temperature or time depending on how your oven works.

basic pan pizza base

This pizza dough makes one large rectangular pizza base, or two 23-cm (9-in) round bases.

125 g (4½ oz) strong white bread flour
160 g (5¼ oz) plain flour
200 ml (7 fl oz) warm water
5 ml (1 tsp) traditional active dried yeast

2.5 ml (½ tsp) clear honey
7.5 ml (1½ tsp) olive oil
4 ml (¾ tsp) salt

To prepare the dough, combine the flour. Place warm water, yeast, honey, and olive oil in bowl of standing mixer. Add 75 g (5 tbsp) flour and mix on low speed or whisk by hand until smooth. Cover with clean paper towel and leave to stand for 20 minutes, until mixture is foamy on top. Add remaining flour and salt and mix with dough hook for 4 minutes, or knead by hand for 10 minutes, until all the flour is incorporated and the dough is smooth. Cover with clean paper towel and place in a warm spot to rise for 1½ hours, or until the dough has almost doubled in volume.

If making one pizza, lightly oil a rectangular baking pan 38.7 x 26 x 1.91 cm (15¼ x 10¼ x ¾in). Place dough in pan, and knock back once in the centre. Using your hands, stretch out the dough from the centre to the sides, taking care to distribute it evenly around the pan. Using cocktail sticks or small lightweight containers as supports in each corner, tent the dough with paper towels and return to warm spot for another 45 minutes.

If making 2 pizzas, lightly oil two 23-cm (9-in) round cake pans. Using your hands or a rolling pin, stretch out each ball to form a 23-cm (9-in) round. With fingers, work a little extra dough to edges to form base. Place dough in pans, cover with clean paper towel, and return to warm spot for 45 minutes.

basic thin pizza base

This base rises only once and bakes in minutes, making it the quickest base to make.
It can be made into three 30-cm (12-in) pizzas, as described below, or divided into
six individual 15-cm (6-in) pizzas. Baking time remains consistent.

175 g (6 oz) plain flour
200 g (7 oz) strong white bread flour
5 ml (1 tsp) sugar
5 ml (1 tsp) easy-blend dried yeast

5 ml (1 tsp) salt
22 ml (1½ tbsp) extra-virgin
  olive oil
225 ml (8 fl oz) very warm water

To prepare the pizza dough, combine flours. Mix 225 g (8 oz) flour with the sugar, yeast, and
salt in bowl of standing mixer. Set aside. Combine olive oil and warm water. With paddle
attachment, slowly stir the water and oil into the flour mixture until well combined.
Mix in the remaining flour.

Change to dough hook attachment and knead on low for 4 to 5 minutes, until dough comes
together as a ball and is smooth and elastic. If not using a standing mixer, turn dough onto
a lightly floured surface and knead by hand for about 10 minutes.

Place dough in lightly oiled bowl and cover with clean paper towel. Set aside in a warm spot
for 1½ to 3 hours, until dough has almost doubled in volume.

Once dough has risen, use a sharp knife to divide the ball into 3 equal pieces. Shape each
into a ball, and flatten to form a disc. Using fingers or rolling pin, stretch out each disc to
30-cm (12-in) rounds, which is very thin — about 2 mm (¹/₁₂ in).

basic calzone dough

This dough is used for all the calzone recipes in this book.

175 g (6 oz) plain flour
200 g (7 oz) strong white bread flour
5 ml (1 tsp) granulated sugar
10 ml (2 tsp) easy-blend dried yeast

5 ml (1 tsp) salt
22 ml (1½ tbsp) extra-virgin
   olive oil
225 ml (8 fl oz) warm water

To prepare the calzone dough, combine flours. Mix 225 g (8 oz) flour with the sugar, yeast, and salt in bowl of standing mixer. Set aside. Combine olive oil and warm water. Using paddle attachment, slowly stir the water and oil into the flour mixture until well combined. Mix in the remaining flour.

Change to dough hook attachment and knead on low for 4 to 5 minutes, until dough comes together as a ball and is smooth and elastic. If not using a standing mixer, turn onto a lightly floured surface and knead by hand for about 10 minutes. Place dough in lightly oiled bowl and cover with clean paper towel. Set aside for 10 minutes.

When the dough has rested for 10 minutes, knock it back. Using a sharp knife, cut the dough into 4 equal pieces. Shape each into a ball, flatten down to form a disc, and lightly flour each disc.

On a lightly floured surface, roll out a 15-cm (6-in) disc, which is about 3 mm (⅛ in) thick. Add flour as necessary to prevent sticking.

basic double pizza base

This is the right base for rustic and other stuffed pizzas.

10 ml (2 tsp) traditional active dried yeast
325 ml (11 fl oz) warm water
225 g (8 oz) plain 2 cups all-purpose flour

200 g (7 oz) strong white bread flour
5 ml (1 tsp) salt

To make the dough, sprinkle yeast over warm water and set aside for a minute, or until yeast becomes foamy. Stir to completely dissolve yeast. Add olive oil to yeast mixture.

Combine flours and salt in large bowl of standing mixer. Add the yeast mixture and, using dough hook attachment, run machine on low speed for 4 to 5 minutes, or until dough forms a ball.

If making dough by hand, stir yeast mixture into flour until dough forms, then turn onto a lightly floured surface and knead for 10 minutes, until the dough is smooth and elastic.

Place dough in lightly oiled bowl and cover with clean paper towel. Set aside in a warm spot for 1½ to 2 hours, until dough has almost doubled in volume.

Knock back dough. Using a sharp knife, cut the dough in 2 pieces, one slightly larger than the other. Shape each piece into a ball. Place balls in lightly floured cake pans, tent the pans with a clean paper towel, and return to warm spot for an additional hour. Dough should almost double in volume again.

basic neapolitan pizza base

A delicious foolproof dough that makes enough for two 30-cm (12-in) pizzas.

5 ml (1 tsp) traditional active dried yeast
300 ml (½ pint) warm water
5 ml (1 tsp) salt
250 g (9 oz) strong white bread flour

115 g (4 oz) plain flour

To prepare the dough, sprinkle yeast over warm water in bowl of standing mixer and set aside for 5 minutes. Add salt, then mix in flour 115 g (4 oz) at a time. When dough is beginning to form, change to dough hook attachment, and run mixer for 4 to 5 minutes, until dough is smooth and elastic.

Divide dough in 2 pieces and place in lightly oiled bowls. Roll dough around so each ball is lightly covered in oil.

Cover bowls with clean paper towels and place in warm spot to rise for 2 to 3 hours, until dough has almost doubled in bulk. If you prefer to make the dough the night before you plan to use it, seal bowls with cling film and place in refrigerator. Remove from refrigerator one hour before you plan to use the dough.

Place pizza stone in oven and preheat oven to the maximum setting, usually 240°C (475°F / Gas Mark 9). Lightly dust each ball with flour. Using fingers or rolling pin, stretch out each ball to form a large circle, roughly 30 cm (12 in) in diameter.

basic turkish pizza base

This dough is used for the Turkish pizza recipe in International Pizzas (page 114), but you can use it for individual pizzas as well. It contains more fat than other pizza doughs, resulting in a slightly softer, more pliable base.

11 g sachet ($2^{1}/_{4}$ tsp) active dried yeast
225 ml (8 fl oz) warm water
30 ml (2 tbsp) unsalted butter, melted
30 ml (2 tbsp) extra virgin olive oil

5 ml (1 tsp) salt
225 g (8 oz) plain flour
125 g ($4^{1}/_{2}$ oz) strong white bread flour

To prepare the dough, sprinkle the yeast over the warm water in large bowl of standing mixer. Stir to mix and set aside for 10 minutes, until yeast has dissolved.

Mix in melted butter and olive oil. Add salt, then mix in flour 115 g (4 oz) at a time. When dough begins to form, change to dough hook attachment, and run mixer for 4 to 5 minutes, until dough is smooth and elastic.

Place dough in lightly oiled bowl. Roll dough around so ball is lightly covered with oil.

Cover bowl with clean paper towel and place in warm spot to rise for 1 hour, until dough has almost doubled in bulk.

Knock back the dough once, cover, and return to the warm spot for 40 minutes.

basic chicago deep-dish pizza base

For all your deep-dish pizza cravings!

2 x 11 g sachets (2¼ tsp each) easy-blend dried
   yeast
500 ml (18 fl oz) warm water
120 ml (4 fl oz) rapeseed oil

60 ml (4 tbsp) olive oil
65 g (2¼ oz) fine cornmeal
10 ml (2 tsp) salt
625 g (1 lb 6 oz) plain flour

To prepare the dough, dissolve yeast over warm water in large bowl of standing mixer. Leave to stand for 2 minutes. Add oil, cornmeal, salt, and 400 g (14 oz) flour. Mix well.

Attach dough hook and mix in remaining flour. Knead for 4 to 5 minutes, until dough is smooth.

Cover bowl with paper towel and place in warm, draught-free spot to rise for 1 hour, until dough has doubled.

Knock back dough once, cover, and return to warm spot for additional 40 minutes. Divide dough into 3 equal pieces and shape each into a ball.

Makes three 23-cm (9-in) bases

basic wholemeal thin pizza base

Wholemeal flour offers more fibre and results in a base with a slightly
coarser texture.

115 g (4 oz) plain flour
125 g (4 1/2 oz) strong white bread flour
125 g (4 1/2 oz) wholemeal flour
5 ml (1 tsp) granulated sugar

5 ml (1 tsp) easy-blend dried yeast
5 ml (1 tsp) salt
22 ml (1 1/2 tbsp) extra-virgin olive oil
225 ml (8 fl oz) very warm water

To prepare the pizza dough, combine the flours. Mix 225 g (8 oz) of the flour with the sugar,
yeast, and salt in bowl of standing mixer. Set aside. Combine olive oil and warm water. With
paddle attachment, slowly stir the water and oil into the flour mixture until well combined.
Mix in the remaining flour.

Change to dough hook attachment and knead on low for 4 to 5 minutes, until dough comes
together as a ball and is smooth and elastic. If not using a standing mixer, turn dough onto
a lightly floured surface and knead by hand for about 10 minutes.

Place dough in lightly oiled bowl and cover with clean paper towel. Set aside in a warm spot
for 1 1/2 to 3 hours, until dough has almost doubled in volume.

Once dough has risen, use a sharp knife to divide the ball into 3 equal pieces. Shape each
into a ball, and flatten to form a disc. Using fingers or rolling pin, stretch out each disc to
30-cm (12- in) rounds, which is very thin – about 2 mm (1/12 in).

basic gluten-free pizza base

This base will make a satisfying pizza base replacement for those who observe a gluten-free diet.

30 ml (2 tbsp) easy-blend dried yeast
5 ml (1 tsp) sugar
325 ml (11 oz) warm milk
200 g (7 oz) brown rice flour
150 g (5¼ oz) tapioca flour

20 ml (4 tsp) guar gum
5 ml (1 tsp) salt
5 ml (2 tsp) powered gelatin
10 ml (2 tsp) extra-virgin olive oil
10 ml (2 tsp) apple cider vinegar

Preheat oven to 220°C (425°F / Gas Mark 7). In small bowl, sprinkle yeast and sugar over warm milk. Set aside for 5 minutes, until yeast and sugar have dissolved. In large bowl of standing mixer, combine flours, guar gum, salt, and gelatin powder. Add yeast mixture and mix until well incorporated. Mix in oil and vinegar.

Cover bowl with cling film and leave to rise for 10 minutes. Line a 30-cm (12-in) pizza pan with baking paper. Turn dough into pizza pan and sprinkle with rice flour.

Using hands, press dough down to cover surface of pan.

Prebake for 10 minutes before adding toppings.

Return to oven with toppings for 15 minutes. Add cheese and bake for 5 minutes longer.

basic pizza sauce

This simple and delicious sauce is used as the base for most pizzas.

45 ml (3 tbsp) olive oil
1 garlic clove, finely chopped
2 x 397 g (14 oz) cans plum tomatoes
2.5 ml (½ tsp) salt

2.5 ml (½ tsp) dried oregano or 15 ml (1 tbsp)
 chopped fresh oregano
pinch of crushed red pepper flakes

To prepare the sauce, heat oil in large heavy frying pan.

Add garlic and cook for 1 to 2 minutes. Add tomatoes and break them up into small chunks with wooden spoon.

Simmer for 15 to 20 minutes, until most of the liquid has evaporated and sauce has thickened. Add salt, oregano, and red pepper flakes to taste.

Makes approximately 400 ml (14 fl oz) sauce

basic pesto

Fresh and fragrant, pesto is easy to make, and it's a delicious addition to pizzas and many flatbreads.

75 g (3 oz) loosely packed fresh basil leaves
25 g (1 oz) pine nuts
25 g (1 oz) finely grated Parmesan
25 g (1 oz) finely grated Pecorino Romano

75 ml (5 tbsp) extra-virgin olive oil
salt and freshly ground black pepper

To make pesto, combine all ingredients except olive oil, salt and pepper in food processor or blender. Run machine until everything is finely chopped. With machine still operating, add olive oil in a thin stream until pesto becomes a smooth pastelike consistency. Season to taste with salt and pepper.

For a bright green pesto that does not discolour, blanche the basil leaves (submerge them in boiling water for a few seconds, until leaves brighten) before proceeding with the recipe.

Leftovers can be refrigerated for up to one week or frozen in ice cube trays for easy thawing. Thawed pesto may need to be returned to the food processor to restore its original texture.

Makes approximately 500 ml (18 fl oz) pesto

basic tapenade

This olive-based spread from Provence makes an appetizing alternative to regular pizza sauce. It can also make a tasty dip for pittas.

115 g (4 oz) anchovy fillets, rinsed and drained
4 peeled garlic cloves
350 g (12 oz) pitted black olives

175 g (6 oz) drained capers
225 ml (8 fl oz) extra-virgin olive oil
juice of 1 lemon

Combine all ingredients except lemon juice and olive oil in food processor. Process until smooth.

With machine running, pour olive oil in a continuous stream through chute.

Add lemon juice. Process until mixture is thick and smooth.

Leftovers may be stored in the fridge for up to one week.

basic sausage sauce

This sauce takes more time to make than the basic pizza sauce, but it is definitely worth the wait! Use hot or mild sausage, according to your tastes.

15 ml (1 tbsp) olive oil
450 g (1 lb) Italian sausage or herby pork
  sausages
2 garlic cloves, crushed
397 g (14 oz) can plum tomatoes

2.5 ml (½ tsp) salt
2.5 ml (½ tsp) dried oregano or 15 ml (1 tbsp)
  chopped fresh oregano
pinch of crushed red pepper flakes

To prepare the sauce, heat oil in large heavy frying pan. Remove sausage from casings and break into small chunks. Add sausage to pan and cook until lightly browned.

Stir in garlic and oregano and cook for 1 to 2 minutes. Add tomatoes and break them up into small chunks with a wooden spoon.

Simmer for at least 1 hour, until most of the liquid has evaporated and sauce has thickened. Add salt and red pepper flakes to taste.

Makes approximately 400 ml (14 fl oz) sauce

basic ratatouille

This Provençal stew makes a delectable pizza topping, especially if you want more vegetables.

45 ml (3 tbsp) extra-virgin olive oil
1 mild onion, chopped
2 small aubergines, ends trimmed and chopped
2 garlic cloves, crushed
3 small courgettes, ends trimmed and chopped
1 green pepper, seeded and chopped
1 red pepper, seeded and chopped

3 fresh thyme sprigs
1 fresh rosemary sprig
1 bay leaf
400 g (14 oz) can plum tomatoes
45 ml (3 tbsp) roughly chopped fresh basil
salt and freshly ground black pepper

In large pan, heat oil over medium heat. Add onion and cook until softened and turning brown, 8 to 10 minutes. Add aubergines and garlic; continue cooking for 4 to 5 minutes. Stir in courgettes and peppers; sauté for 5 minutes.

Place thyme, rosemary, and bay leaf in a small muslin bag, or simply tie together with kitchen string to make a bouquet garni.

Add the tomatoes and bouquet garni to the pan, and reduce heat to medium low. Cover saucepan and simmer for 30 to 40 minutes, stirring occasionally.

Remove bouquet garni and bay leaf. Stir in basil and season to taste.

pan pizzas

With a thick base (soft inside and crispy outside) and layers of tomato sauce, melted cheese and delicious toppings, these pan pizzas will please a crowd or satisfy a hungry family.

classic cheese pizza

see variations page 48

When you want a classic, this is where to start!

1 recipe basic pan pizza base
    (page 16)
1 recipe basic pizza sauce
    (page 25)
175 g (6 oz) grated mozzarella

Follow the instructions on page 16 for making a rectangular pizza base.

Preheat oven to the maximum setting, usually 240°C (475°F / Gas Mark 9). Spread sauce evenly over the pizza base, leaving a 1-cm (¹/₂-in) border around the edge. Place on bottom rack in oven and bake for 8 minutes. Remove from oven and spread grated mozzarella evenly over sauce.

Return to oven and bake for another 5 to 6 minutes, until cheese has melted and base is golden brown.

Remove from oven and leave to stand for 5 minutes. Slice into 12 squares and serve immediately.

Makes 1 large rectangular pizza. Serves 6–8.

grilled chicken & fontina pizza

see variations page 49

This is an excellent way to add appeal to leftover grilled chicken.

1 recipe basic pan pizza base (page 16)
$\frac{1}{2}$ recipe basic pizza sauce (page 25)
225 g (8 oz) grated Fontina cheese
1-2 grilled and sliced chicken breasts

2 thin slices red onion, rings separated
freshly ground black pepper
30 ml (2 tbsp) finely chopped flat-leaf parsley
60 ml (4 tbsp) finely grated Parmesan

Follow the instructions on page 16 for making 2 round pizza bases.

Preheat oven to the maximum setting, usually 240°C (475°F / Gas Mark 9). Divide the sauce between the 2 pans and spread thinly and evenly, leaving 1-cm ($\frac{1}{2}$-in) border around the edge.

Spread half the grated Fontina over the sauce on each pizza. Arrange half the onion rings and half the chicken on each pizza. Lightly sprinkle each one with pepper.

Bake for 8 to 10 minutes on middle rack in oven, until cheese is melted and base is golden brown. Sprinkle chopped parsley and Parmesan over pizzas.

Slice into wedges and serve.

Makes two 23-cm (9-in) pizzas. Serves 6–8.

pizza margherita

see variations page 50

Invented in 1889 and named after Queen Margherita, this pizza features the three colours of the Italian flag – red (tomatoes), white (mozzarella) and green (basil).

1 recipe basic pan pizza base (page 16)
1 recipe basic pizza sauce (page 25)
115 g (4 oz) baby bocconcini, sliced thin
    (or sliced mozzarella)
4 large basil leaves, roughly torn

Follow the instructions on page 16 for making 2 round pizza bases.

Preheat oven to the maximum setting, usually 240°C (475°F / Gas Mark 9). Divide sauce between the 2 pans and spread evenly, leaving 1-cm ($\frac{1}{2}$-in) border around the edge.

Distribute cheese slices around the 2 pizzas.

Bake for 8 to 10 minutes on rack in lower half of oven, until cheese is melted and base is golden brown. Sprinkle pieces of basil over pizzas.

Slice into wedges and serve.

Makes two 23-cm (9-in) pizzas. Serves 6–8.

sausage & pepper pizza

see variations page 51

Spicy sausage chunks and red pepper slices make this pizza burst with flavour.

1 recipe basic pan pizza base (page 16)
450 g (1 lb) mild or hot Italian sausage, pork
    sausage with fennel or herby pork sausage
15 ml (1 tbsp) olive oil

1 recipe basic pizza sauce (page 25)
225 g (8 oz) grated mozzarella
1 red pepper, seeded and thinly
    sliced crossways

Follow the instructions on page 16 for making a rectangular pizza base.

Preheat oven to the maximum setting, usually 240°C (475°F / Gas Mark 9). Remove sausage meat from casings and shape into small chunks. Heat olive oil in large skillet and brown sausage. Remove sausage from pan and drain. Spread sauce evenly over the pizza base, leaving a 1-cm ($\frac{1}{2}$-in) border around the edge.

Place on bottom rack in oven and bake for 8 minutes. Remove from oven and spread grated mozzarella evenly over sauce. Arrange sausage chunks and red pepper slices on top. Return to oven and bake for another 5 to 6 minutes, until cheese has melted and base is golden brown.

Remove from oven and leave to stand for 5 minutes. Slice into 12 squares and serve immediately.

Makes 1 large rectangular pizza. Serves 6–8.

vegetarian pizza

see variations page 52

Overflowing with fresh tomatoes, mushrooms, onions, peppers, and green and black olives, this pizza is a vegetable lover's dream.

1 recipe basic pan pizza base
   (page 16)
1 recipe basic pizza sauce
   (page 25)
225 g (8 oz) grated mozzarella

2-3 vine-ripened tomatoes,
   sliced
115 g (4 oz) sliced mushrooms
1 mild onion, thinly sliced
1 green pepper, thinly sliced

50 g (2 oz) pitted sliced
   Manzanilla olives
50 g (2 oz) pitted sliced black
   olives

Follow the instructions on page 16 for making a rectangular pizza base.

Preheat oven to the maximum setting, usually 240°C (475°F / Gas Mark 9). Spread sauce evenly over the pizza base, leaving a 1-cm (1/2-in) border around the edge. Place on bottom rack in oven and bake for 8 minutes.

Remove from the oven and spread grated mozzarella evenly over sauce. Arrange the fresh tomato, mushroom, onion, pepper, and olive slices over cheese. Return to oven and bake for another 5 to 6 minutes, until the cheese has melted and base is golden brown.

Remove from the oven and leave to stand for 5 minutes. Slice into 12 squares and serve immediately.

Makes 1 large rectangular pizza. Serves 6–8.

classic pan pizza with the works

see variations page 53

"Pizza with the works" traditionally refers to pizza with the combination of cheese, pepperoni, onion, mushrooms, and green peppers. Try some of our variations for tasty extras.

1 recipe basic pan pizza base (page 16)
1 recipe basic pizza sauce (page 25)
225 g (8 oz) grated mozzarella

225 g (8 oz) Pepperoni, thinly sliced (about 24 thin slices)
225 g (8 oz) button mushrooms, sliced

½ large mild onion, thinly sliced
1 large green pepper, seeded and thinly sliced crossways

Follow the instructions on page 16 for making a rectangular pizza base.

Preheat oven to the maximum setting, usually 240°C (475°F / Gas Mark 9). Spread sauce evenly over the pizza base, leaving a 1-cm (½-in) border around the edge. Place on bottom rack in oven and bake for 8 minutes.

Remove from oven and spread grated mozzarella evenly over sauce. Arrange pepperoni, onion, mushroom, and pepper slices on top.

Return to oven and bake for another 5 to 6 minutes, until cheese has melted and base is golden brown. Remove from oven and leave to stand for 5 minutes.

Slice into 12 squares and serve immediately.
Makes 1 large rectangular pizza. Serves 6–8.

garlic & olive oil pizza

see variations page 54

Slice this pizza in fingers and serve as an alternative to garlic bread.

1 recipe basic pan pizza base (page 16)
2 garlic cloves, finely chopped
30 ml (2 tbsp) extra-virgin olive oil

2.5 ml (½ tsp) dried oregano
pinch of crushed red pepper flakes
pinch of coarse salt

Follow the instructions on page 16 for making 2 round pizza bases.

Preheat oven to the maximum setting, usually 240°C (475°F / Gas Mark 9). Combine the garlic, olive oil, oregano, red pepper flakes and salt. Divide the mixture between the 2 pizzas.

Spread the sauce around, leaving 1-cm (½-in) border.

Bake on bottom rack in oven for 7 to 9 minutes, until base is golden brown. Leave to stand for 5 minutes, slice into wedges or fingers, and serve.

Makes two 23-cm (9-in) pizzas. Serves 6–8.

steak & mushroom pizza

see variations page 55

This hearty pizza is guaranteed to satisfy the biggest appetites!

1 recipe basic pan pizza base (page 16)
1 recipe basic pizza sauce (page 25)
350 g (12 oz) lightly grilled sirloin steak, thinly sliced
225 g (8 oz) white or brown mushrooms, thinly sliced

115 g (4 oz) grated mozzarella cheese
115 g (4 oz) grated smoked Gruyère cheese
2.5 ml (½ tsp) dried oregano (optional)

Follow the instructions on page 16 for making 2 round pizza bases.

Preheat oven to the maximum setting, usually 240°C (475°F / Gas Mark 9). Divide sauce between the 2 pans and spread evenly, leaving 1-cm (½-in) border around the edge. Arrange steak and mushroom slices on both pizzas.

Combine the grated cheeses and divide evenly between the 2 pans.

Bake for 8 to 10 minutes on rack in lower half of oven, until cheese is melted and base is golden brown. Sprinkle with oregano if desired.

Slice into wedges and serve.

Makes two 9-in (23-cm) pizzas. Serves 6–8.

caramelized onion, anchovy & olive pizza

see variations page 56

The sweetness of the caramelized onions offers the perfect complement to the salty anchovies and olives in this sophisticated pizza.

1 recipe basic pan pizza base (page 16)
60-75 ml (4-5 tbsp) extra-virgin olive oil
4 mild onions, thinly sliced
50 g (2 oz) butter

1.25 ml ($^1/_4$ tsp) crumbled, dried rosemary
salt and freshly ground black pepper
8-10 drained canned anchovies

50 g (2 oz) pitted Kalamata olives
50 g (2 oz) grated Pecorino Romano cheese

Follow the instructions on page 16 for making a rectangular pizza base.

Preheat oven to the maximum setting, usually 240°C (475°F / Gas Mark 9). Warm the oil in a large heavy skillet. Add the onions. Cook for 5 minutes or until onions soften. Add butter and rosemary and cook over low heat for 15 minutes, or until onions have caramelized. Add pinch of salt and pepper; leave to cool. Spread caramelized onions over pizza dough, leaving 1-cm ($^1/_2$-in) border around the edge. Arrange anchovies and olives on top. Bake on bottom rack in oven for 8 minutes. Remove from oven and sprinkle with grated Pecorino cheese. Return to oven and bake for another 5 to 6 minutes, until cheese has melted and base is golden brown. Remove from oven and leave to stand for 5 minutes. Slice into 12 squares and serve immediately.

Makes 1 large rectangular pizza. Serves 6–8.

seafood pizza

see variations page 57

This exquisite pizza needs only a mixed green salad to complete it.

1 recipe basic pan pizza base (page 16)
30 ml (2 tbsp) extra-virgin olive oil
1 garlic clove, finely chopped
150 g (5 oz) cleaned calamari, thawed if frozen
12-15 medium shelled prawns, thawed if
    frozen, deveined

12-15 shelled mussels
salt and freshly ground black pepper
30 ml (2 tbsp) chopped flat-leaf parsley
10 ml (2 tsp) finely grated lemon rind

Follow the instructions on page 16 for making a rectangular pizza base.

Preheat oven to the maximum setting, usually 240°C (475°F / Gas Mark 9). Heat olive oil in large nonstick skillet. Add garlic and cook for 1 minute. Add seafood and cook for 1 to 2 minutes, until prawns have turned pink and calamari rings are opaque. Spread seafood around pizzas, leaving 1-cm (½-in) border.

Sprinkle with salt and freshly ground black pepper. Bake on middle rack in oven for 8 to 10 minutes, until base is golden brown.

Leave to stand for 5 minutes. Sprinkle with parsley and grated lemon rind. Slice into wedges and serve immediately.

Makes two 23-cm (9-in) pizzas. Serves 6–8.

variations

classic cheese pizza

see base recipe page 31

pepperoni & cheese pizza
Prepare the basic recipe, adding 12 to 14 thin slices (115 g / 4 oz) of pepperoni over the sauce before adding the cheese.

salami & cheese pizza
Prepare the basic recipe, adding 3 to 4 slices of salami, quartered into triangles, over the grated cheese.

prosciutto & cheese pizza
Prepare the basic recipe, adding 3 to 4 slices prosciutto, torn into strips, over the sauce before adding the cheese.

pancetta & cheese pizza
Prepare the basic recipe, adding 50 g (2 oz) pancetta, cubed and fried until crisp, over the shredded cheese.

parma ham & cheese pizza
Prepare the basic recipe, adding 3 to 4 slices Parma ham, torn into strips, over the sauce before adding the cheese.

variations

grilled chicken & fontina pizza

see base recipe page 32

bbq chicken & fontina pizza
Prepare the basic recipe, replacing the grilled chicken with an equal quantity of shredded rotisserie-barbecued chicken.

grilled chicken with sun-dried tomato pizza
Prepare the basic recipe, adding 4 drained and roughly chopped large sun-dried tomatoes (2 per pizza) over the layer of sauce. Omit the red onion slices if desired.

grilled chicken & pesto pizza
Prepare the basic recipe, replacing the basic tomato sauce with 60 ml (4 tbsp) pesto (see page 26) per pizza. Omit Fontina cheese, red onion slices, and parsley. Garnish cooked pizza with 25 g (1 oz) toasted pine nuts, if desired.

jerk chicken with cheese pizza
Prepare the basic recipe, replacing grilled chicken with an equal quantity of cooked and shredded jerk or Cajun-style chicken. Replace Fontina cheese with an equal quantity of grated cheddar or Monterey Jack cheese and substitute fresh coriander for the parsley.

grilled chicken with crispy onion pizza
Prepare the basic recipe, replacing the red onion slices with a generous sprinkling of shop bought crispy onion topping.

variations

pizza margherita

see base recipe page 35

pizza margherita on gluten-free pizza base
Prepare the basic recipe, replacing the Basic Pan Pizza Base with the Gluten-Free Pizza Base (page 24).

pizza margherita with anchovies
Prepare the basic recipe, placing pieces of dried anchovies (approximately 6 pieces per pizza) over the sauce before adding the cheese.

pizza margherita with artichoke hearts
Prepare the basic recipe, adding 75 g (3 oz) chopped drained marinated artichoke hearts to each pizza, before adding the cheese.

pizza margherita with olives
Prepare the basic recipe, adding 50 g (2 oz) chopped drained pitted marinated olives to each pizza, before adding the cheese.

pizza margherita with chèvre
Prepare the basic recipe, replacing the bocconcini with an equal quantity of sliced chèvre (goat's cheese).

variations

sausage & pepper pizza

see base recipe page 36

sausage & sauerkraut pizza
Prepare the basic recipe, replacing the red pepper slices with 65 g (2½ oz) drained canned sauerkraut.

sausage pizza with mushroom ragout
Prepare the basic recipe, replacing the red pepper slices with 120 ml (4 fl oz) prepared creamed mushrooms.

sausage & pepper pizza with three onions
Prepare the basic recipe, replacing the red pepper slices with a mixture of mild white onion slices, red onion slices and spring onion slices.

sausage & chutney pizza
Prepare the basic recipe, replacing the basic pizza sauce with 350 ml (12 fl oz) chutney.

sausage & pepper pizza on gluten-free base
Prepare the basic recipe, replacing the Basic Pan Pizza Base with the Gluten-Free Pizza Base (page 24).

vegetarian pizza

see base recipe page 39

vegetarian pizza with asparagus
Prepare the basic recipe, adding 8 to 10 spears steamed asparagus with the other toppings.

vegetarian pizza with feta
Prepare the basic recipe, replacing the mozzarella with 350 g (12 oz) crumbled feta.

vegetarian pizza with leeks
Prepare the basic recipe, adding 1 leek, which has been cut into matchsticks and steamed until tender, with the other toppings.

vegetarian pizza with roasted root vegetables, pesto & chèvre
Prepare the basic recipe, replacing the basic tomato sauce with 120 ml (4 fl oz) prepared pesto. Replace mozzarella with 275 g (10 oz) crumbled soft unripened chèvre (goat's cheese). Omit the sliced tomatoes, mushrooms, onions, peppers, and olives. Replace with about 425 g (15 oz) assorted roasted root vegetables, such as carrots, parsnips, and beetroots.

vegetarian pizza with smoked gruyère
Prepare the basic recipe, replacing half of the mozzarella with smoked Gruyère. Mix the cheeses together before sprinkling them over the sauce.

variations

classic pan pizza with the works

see base recipe page 40

pizza with the works & bacon
Prepare the basic recipe, crumbling 4 slices crisp fried bacon over the pizza with the other toppings.

pizza with the works & three peppers
Prepare the basic recipe, using only ½ green pepper, and adding thin slices of ½ yellow and ½ red pepper with the other toppings.

pizza with the works & sausage
Prepare the basic recipe, but add to the other toppings 225 g (8 oz) spicy or herb sausage meat, shaped into small chunks, browned in 15 ml (1 tbsp) olive oil, and drained.

pizza with the works & roast beef
Prepare the basic recipe, omitting the pepperoni and adding 225 g (8 oz) sliced deli or leftover roast beef with the other toppings.

pizza with the works & cheese base
Prepare the basic recipe, lightly glazing the edge of the base with olive oil and sprinkling it with an additional 25 g (1 oz) grated mozzarella when adding the rest of the cheese.

variations

garlic & olive oil pizza

see base recipe page 43

garlic & olive oil pizza with flat-leaf parsley
Prepare the basic recipe, sprinkling 30 ml (2 tbsp) fresh chopped flat-leaf
parsley over each pizza after they have been removed from the oven.

garlic & olive oil pizza with cheese
Prepare the basic recipe, adding 175 g (6 oz) grated mozzarella over each
pizza after 5 minutes baking. Return to oven for additional 3 to 5 minutes,
until cheese is melted and base is golden brown.

garlic & olive oil pizza with kalamata olives
Prepare the basic recipe, adding 50 ml (2 oz) halved and pitted kalamata
olives to each pizza, after spreading the sauce.

garlic & olive oil pizza with prawn
Prepare the basic recipe, adding 50 g (2 oz) deveined, peeled, and cooked
prawn to each pizza, after spreading the sauce.

garlic & olive oil pizza with sesame seed base
Prepare the basic recipe, lightly glazing each base with olive oil
and sprinkling with 5 ml (1 tbsp) sesame seeds before adding sauce.

variations

steak & mushroom pizza

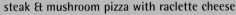

see base recipe page 44

steak & mushroom pizza with raclette cheese
Prepare the basic recipe, replacing the smoked Gruyère cheese with
an equal quantity of grated aclette cheese.

steak & mushroom pizza with onions
Prepare the basic recipe, adding ½ thinly sliced red onion with the
steak and mushrooms.

steak & aubergine pizza
Prepare the basic recipe, replacing the mushrooms with 1 small Italian
aurbergine, which has been sliced and grilled.

steak & zucchini pizza
Prepare the basic recipe, replacing the mushrooms with 1 small courgette,
which has been sliced lengthways and grilled.

steak & mushroom pizza with herb base
Prepare the basic recipe, lightly glazing the edge of the base with olive oil
and sprinkling with 2.5 ml (½ tsp) Italian seasoning before adding the sauce.

variations

caramelized onion, anchovy & olive pizza

see base recipe page 45

caramelized onion & boursin pizza
Prepare the basic recipe, but replace the Pecorino with 275 g (10 oz) Boursin (a soft herb cheese), in small chunks, scattered over the caramelized onions, anchovies, and olives.

caramelized onion & gorgonzola pizza
Prepare the basic recipe, but replace the Pecorino with 275 g (10 oz) Gorgonzola, in small chunks, scattered over the caramelized onions, anchovies and olives.

caramelized onion & mushroom pizza
Prepare the basic recipe, adding 115 g (4 oz) sliced mushrooms to the onions to be caramelized.

caramelized onion with smoked mackerel pizza
Prepare the basic recipe, replacing the anchovies with 225 g (8 oz) smoked mackerel, roughly broken into pieces. Omit the olives.

anchovy, olive & tomato pizza
Prepare the basic recipe, omitting caramelized onions. Lightly glaze base with extra-virgin olive oil and add 1 to 2 thinly sliced fresh tomatoes with the anchovies and olives.

seafood pizza

see base recipe page 46

mussel pizza with roasted garlic

Prepare the basic recipe, omitting prawn and squid, and doubling the quantity of mussls. To prepare roasted garlic, place 3 heads of garlic, drizzled with olive oil, on a baking pan in a preheated 190°C (375°F / Gas Mark 5) oven for 50 to 60 minutes. Leave to cool, and slice in half crossways, between stem and base of bulbs. Squeeze roasted garlic into bowl, add olive oil from pan, and mash with fork until smooth. Spread 30-45 ml (2-3 tbsp) garlic purée over each base before adding the mussels. Sprinkle with dried oregano and 30 ml (2 tbsp) grated Romano Pecorino cheese.

seafood pizza with tomatoes

Prepare the basic recipe, arranging 1 sliced tomato on top before adding seafood.

crab & chèvre pizza

Prepare the basic recipe, replacing seafood mixture with 200 g (7 oz) crabmeat mixed with 150 g (5 oz) soft, unripened chèvre (goat's cheese). Top with 2 diced and seeded plum tomatoes, and chopped Kalamata olives if desired.

calamari pizza

Prepare the basic recipe, omitting prawns and mussels. Double quantity of calamari. Once calamari is arranged on base, dot with 50-115 g (2-4 oz) soft, unripened chèvre (goat's cheese); sprinkle with dried oregano and chopped Kalamata olives if desired.

thin base pizzas

These pizzas make elegant appetisers, speedy snacks or great meals – the base bakes quickly so they are ready before you know it. Spread out an assortment of toppings and let friends and family choose their own for an informal pizza night – the base is popular with adults and kids alike.

spinach & feta pizza

see variations page 76

Creamy spinach makes a great alternative to tomato sauce.

1 recipe basic thin pizza base (page 17)
450 g (1 lb) baby spinach
22 ml (1½ tbsp) extra-virgin olive oil
1 garlic clove, finely chopped
115 g (4 oz) ricotta cheese

2.5 ml (½ tsp) dried oregano
pinch of ground nutmeg
salt and freshly ground black pepper
250 g (9 oz) crumbled feta cheese

Preheat oven to the maximum setting, usually 240°C (475°F / Gas Mark 9). Place a pizza stone or unglazed clay tiles on the bottom of gas oven or lowest rack of electric oven. Following instructions on page 17, make three 30-cm (12-in) discs of pizza dough. To make spinach topping, remove stems from spinach. Heat oil in large, heavy skillet over medium heat. Add finely chopped garlic and cook for 1 minute. Add spinach and toss until all the leaves have wilted. Leave to cool, and wrap in paper towels to squeeze out excess moisture. In a medium bowl, combine spinach and ricotta until smooth. Season with oregano, nutmeg, and salt and pepper to taste. Lightly dust pizza peel with flour or cornmeal. Place one disc of pizza dough on peel and spread ⅓ of the spinach over the dough, leaving 1-cm (½-in) border around the edge. Sprinkle with ⅓ of the crumbled feta and gently shake pizza from the peel to the stone or tiles. Bake for 5 to 7 minutes, until cheese is melting and base is puffy around edges and crisp on the bottom. Slide the peel back under the pizza to remove from oven. Repeat with remaining 2 pizzas.

Makes three 30-cm (12-in) pizzas. Serves 6.

garden vegetable pizza

see variations page 77

The perfect pizza to make when gardens and markets are filled with beautiful produce.

1 recipe basic thin pizza base
(page 17)
1 large aubergine, sliced
crossways
275 g (10 oz) courgettes,
trimmed and sliced

15-30 ml (1–2 tbsp) extra-
virgin olive oil
salt and freshly ground
black pepper
1 recipe basic pizza sauce
(page 25)

2 large fresh tomatoes, sliced
225 g (8 oz) Boursin (soft
unripened herb cheese)
30 ml (2 tbsp) finely chopped
fresh mixed herbs (basil,
oregano, rosemary)

Preheat oven to the maximum setting, usually 240°C (475°F / Gas Mark 9). Place pizza stone
or unglazed clay tiles on bottom of gas oven or lowest rack of electric oven. Following
instructions on page 17, make three 30-cm (12-in) discs of pizza dough. To prepare the
vegetables, heat grill pan or barbecue grill to medium-high heat. Working in batches, place
aubergine and courgette slices in pan or on grill, brush lightly with olive oil, and cook each
side for 3 to 4 minutes, until vegetables are tender and grill-marked. Season with salt and
pepper and set aside. Lightly dust pizza peel with flour or cornmeal. Place one disc of pizza
dough on peel and spread ⅓ of the pizza sauce over the dough, leaving 1-cm (½-in) border
around the edge. Arrange several slices of aubergine, courgettes and tomato over sauce. Dot
with small chunks of Boursin and sprinkle with 1 teaspoon fresh herbs. Gently shake pizza
from the peel to the stone or tiles. Bake for 5 to 7 minutes, until cheese is melting and base
is puffy around edges and crisp on the bottom. Slide the peel back under the pizza to remove
from oven and sprinkle with 5 ml (1 tsp) chopped fresh herbs. Repeat with remaining 2 pizzas.

Makes three 30-cm (12-in) pizzas. Serves 6.

pesto pizza

see variations page 78

Such a simple pizza, yet totally divine.

1 recipe basic thin pizza base (page 17)
175 ml (6 fl oz) basic pesto (page 26)
2 fresh tomatoes, thinly sliced
175 g (6 oz) grated mozzarella

Preheat oven to the maximum setting, usually 240°C (475°F / Gas Mark 9). Place pizza stone or unglazed clay tiles on bottom of gas oven or lowest rack of electric oven.

Following instructions on page 17, make three 30-cm (12-in) discs of pizza dough. Lightly dust pizza peel with flour or cornmeal.

Place one 30-cm (12-in) disc of pizza dough on peel and spread 60 ml (4 tbsp) cup pesto over the dough, leaving a 1-cm (1/2-in) border around the edge.

Arrange 6 to 8 slices of tomato and sprinkle 1/3 of the grated mozzarella on top. Gently shake pizza from the peel to the stone or tiles.

Bake for 4 to 6 minutes, until cheese is melting and base is puffy around edges and crisp on the bottom. Slide the peel back under the pizza to remove from oven. Repeat with remaining 2 pizzas.

Makes three 30-cm (12-in) pizzas. Serves 6.

wild mushrooms on wholemeal pizza base

see variations page 79

The earthy flavours of mixed mushrooms pairs perfectly with the wholemeal base.

1 recipe basic thin whole-wheat base (page 23)
1 recipe basic pizza sauce (page 25)
15 ml (1 tbsp) extra-virgin olive oil
3 garlic cloves finely chopped
900 g (2 lb) assorted wild mushrooms (shiitake, oyster, field and portobello), wiped clean, stemmed, and sliced

675 g (1½ lb) button mushrooms, wiped clean, stemmed, and sliced
2.5 ml (½ tsp) crumbled dried rosemary
175 g (6 oz) grated mozzarella cheese

Preheat oven to the maximum setting, usually 240°C (475°F / Gas Mark 9). Place a pizza stone or unglazed clay tiles on bottom of gas oven or lowest rack of electric oven. Following instructions on page 23, make three 30-cm (12-in) discs of pizza dough. Heat olive oil in large, heavy skillet. Add garlic and cook for 1 minute. Add mushrooms and continue cooking for 15 minutes, until liquid has evaporated and mushrooms are tender. Lightly dust pizza peel with flour or cornmeal. Place one disc of pizza dough on peel and spread ⅓ of the pizza sauce over the dough, leaving 1-cm (½-in) border around the edge. Spread ⅓ of the mushroom mixture over the sauce, sprinkle with rosemary, and arrange ⅓ of the grated mozzarella on top. Gently shake pizza from the peel to the stone or tiles. Bake for 4 to 6 minutes, until cheese is melting and base is puffy around edges and crisp on the bottom. Slide the peel back under the pizza to remove from oven. Repeat with remaining 2 pizzas.

Makes three 30-cm (12-in) pizzas. Serves 6.

four seasons pizza

see variations page 80

A visually stunning pizza that truly evokes the flavours of each season.

1 recipe basic thin pizza base (page 17)
Spring topping
450 g (1 lb) fresh asparagus, ends trimmed
Winter topping
225 g (8 oz) ricotta cheese
25 g (1 oz) finely grated Parmesan
pinch of grated nutmeg
salt and freshly ground pepper

Summer topping
225 g (8 fl oz) pesto (page 26)
Autumn topping
225 g (8 fl oz) red pepper hummus

Preheat oven to the maximum setting, usually 240°C (475°F / Gas Mark 9). Place pizza stone or unglazed clay tiles on bottom of gas oven or lowest rack of electric oven. Following instructions on page 17, make three 30-cm (12-in) discs of pizza dough. To prepare spring topping, steam asparagus for 4 to 5 minutes until chrisp-tender. To prepare winter topping, combine ricotta, Parmesan, nutmeg, salt, and pepper in bowl. Lightly dust pizza peel with flour or cornmeal. Place one disc of pizza dough on peel and spread 1/3 of the ricotta mixture over 1/4 of the pizza surface, leaving 1-cm (1/2-in) border around the edge. Place 1/3 of the asparagus stalks over the next quarter, trimming the ends as necessary so each stalk fits nicely. Spread 1/3 of the pesto over third quarter and 1/3 of the red pepper hummus over the final quarter. Gently shake pizza from the peel to the stone or tiles. Bake for 4 to 6 minutes, until base is puffy around edges and crisp on the bottom. Slide the peel back under the pizza to remove from oven. Repeat with remaining 2 pizzas.

Makes three 30-cm (12-in) pizzas. Serves 6.

pizza bianca

see variations page 81

This twist on the classic white pizza hides wilted spinach between two sumptuous layers of cheese.

1 recipe basic thin pizza base (page 17)
450 g (1 lb) ricotta cheese
30 ml (2 tbsp) finely chopped fresh basil

salt and freshly ground black pepper
pinch of grated nutmeg
75 g (3 oz) wilted and chopped spinach leaves

275 g (9 oz) grated mozzarella cheese
40 g (1½ oz) finely grated Parmesan

Preheat oven to the maximum setting, usually 240°C (475°F / Gas Mark 9). Place pizza stone or unglazed clay tiles on bottom of gas oven or lowest rack of electric oven. Following instructions on page 17, make three 30-cm (12-in) discs of pizza dough.

To prepare topping, combine ricotta and basil in a medium bowl. Season with salt, pepper, and nutmeg. Lightly dust pizza peel with flour or cornmeal. Place one disc of pizza dough on peel and spread ⅓ of the ricotta mixture over the dough, leaving 1-cm (½-in) border around the edge. Arrange ⅓ of the spinach over ricotta and top with ⅓ of the grated mozzarella and ⅓ of the Parmesan. Gently shake pizza from the peel to the stone or tiles.

Bake for 4 to 6 minutes, until cheese is melting and base is puffy around edges and crisp on the bottom. Slide the peel back under the pizza to remove from oven. Repeat with remaining 2 pizzas.

Makes three 30-cm (12-in) pizzas. Serves 6.

tapenade pizza

see variations page 82

Tapenade, a rich dip originating from Provence, is traditionally made with black olives, capers, and anchovies. Variations can be found in gourmet and speciality food shops.

1 recipe basic thin pizza base (page 17)
350 ml (12 fl oz) basic tapenade (page 27)
175 g (6 oz) chèvre (goat's cheese)

Preheat oven to the maximum setting, usually 240°C (475°F / Gas Mark 9). Place pizza stone or unglazed clay tiles on bottom of gas oven or lowest rack of electric oven.

Following instructions on page 17, make three 30-cm (12-in) discs of pizza dough. Lightly dust pizza peel with flour or cornmeal. Place one disc of pizza dough on peel and spread 120 ml (4 fl oz) tapenade over the dough, leaving 1-cm (½-in) border around the edge.

Distribute the chèvre, in 2.5 ml (½ tsp) chunks, over the tapenade. Gently shake the pizza from the peel to the stone or tiles.

Bake for 4 to 5 minutes, until cheese is melting and base is puffy around edges and crisp on the bottom. Slide the peel back under the pizza to remove from oven. Repeat with remaining 2 pizzas.

Makes three 30-cm (12-in) pizzas. Serves 6.

smoked salmon & caper pizza

see variations page 83

The base for this pizza bakes before you add the toppings, making it easy to assemble for a breakfast buffet or to serve in wedges as hors d'oeuvres.

1 recipe basic thin pizza base (page 17)
225 g (8 oz) cream cheese
120 g (4 fl oz) sour cream
15 ml (1 tbsp) chopped fresh dill

5 ml (1 tsp) lemon juice
350 g (12 oz) smoked salmon
90 ml (6 tbsp) drained capers

Preheat oven to the maximum setting, usually 240°C (475°F / Gas Mark 9). Place pizza stone or unglazed clay tiles on bottom of gas oven or lowest rack of electric oven.

Following instructions on page 17, make three 30-cm (12-in) discs of pizza dough. Lightly dust pizza peel with flour or cornmeal. Place one disc of pizza dough on peel and gently shake pizza from the peel to the stone or tiles.

Bake for 4 to 5 minutes. Leave to stand until pizza is cool to the touch.

To prepare the cream cheese spread, combine cream cheese, sour cream, dill, and lemon juice until smooth. Spread ⅓ of the cream cheese mixture over each pizza. Top each pizza with 115 g (4 oz) smoked salmon and 30 ml (2 tbsp) capers.

Repeat with remaining 2 pizzas.

Makes three 30-cm (12-in) pizzas. Serves 6.

fresh tomato pizza

see variations page 84

This pizza should only be made with vine-ripened tomatoes in season and, ideally, eaten al fresco!

1 recipe basic thin pizza base
  (page 17)
4 vine-ripened tomatoes,
  roughly chopped
4–5 fresh basil leaves, torn

1 clove garlic, finely chopped
30 ml (2 tbsp) extra-virgin
  olive oil
salt and freshly ground black
  pepper

225 g (8 oz) grated mozzarella
  cheese
2 vine-ripened tomatoes,
  thinly sliced
30 ml (2 tbsp) finely chopped

Preheat oven to the maximum setting, usually 240°C (475°F / Gas Mark 9). Place pizza stone or unglazed clay tiles on bottom of gas oven or lowest rack of electric oven.

Following instructions on page 17, make three 30-cm (12-in) discs of pizza dough.

To make fresh tomato sauce, use hand-held or traditional blender to purée chopped tomatoes, basil, garlic, and olive oil. Season with salt and pepper. Lightly dust pizza peel with flour or cornmeal. Place one disc of pizza dough on peel and spread $1/3$ of the sauce over the base. Sprinkle $1/3$ of the grated mozzarella over the sauce. Arrange the fresh tomato slices over the cheese. Gently shake pizza from the peel to the stone or tiles.

Bake for 4 to 5 minutes. Sprinkle 10 ml (2 tsp) chopped basil over the pizza. Repeat with remaining 2 pizzas.

Makes three 30-cm (12-in) pizzas. Serves 6.

chèvre, rocket & pear pizza

see variations page 85

The unusual combination of flavours makes this a remarkably refreshing pizza.

1 recipe basic thin pizza base (page 17)
350 g (12 oz) chèvre (goat's cheese)
60 ml (4 tbsp) crème fraiche
3 firm, ripe pears, such as Williams or
    Conference, peeled, cored and sliced

10 ml (2 tsp) lemon juice
225 g (8 oz) baby rocket leaves, cleaned,
    dried and stemmed

Preheat oven to the maximum setting, usually 240°C (475°F / Gas Mark 9). Place pizza stone
or unglazed clay tiles on bottom of gas oven or lowest rack of electric oven.

Following instructions on page 17, make three 30-cm (12-in) discs of pizza dough.
Lightly dust pizza peel with flour or cornmeal and place one disc of pizza dough on peel.

In a bowl, combine chèvre and crème fraiche until smooth. Toss pear slices in lemon juice
to prevent discoloration. Spread $1/3$ of the chèvre mixture over base, leaving a 1-cm
($1/2$-in) border around the edge. Arrange slices from 1 pear over chèvre mixture. Place
$1/3$ rocket leaves over the pear slices. Gently shake the pizza from the peel to the
stone or tiles.

Bake for 4 to 5 minutes. Repeat with remaining 2 pizzas.

Makes three 30-cm (12-in) pizzas. Serves 6.

spinach & feta pizza

see base recipe page 59

spinach, feta & sun-dried tomato pizza

Prepare the basic recipe, adding 2 large sun-dried tomatoes, drained
and chopped, to each pizza with the feta.

spinach, bacon & chèvre pizza

Prepare the basic recipe. Fry 12 slices bacon until crisp, then drain, crumble,
and divide into 3 portions. Add 1 portion to each pizza. Replace crumbled
feta with an equal quantity of chèvre (goat's cheese).

spinach, feta & olive pizza

Prepare the basic recipe, adding 50 g (2 oz) drained and chopped black olives
to each pizza with the feta.

creamy spinach & egg pizza

Prepare the basic recipe, reducing oven to 200°C (400°F / Gas Mark 6). Cream
the spinach mixture in a food mill or with a hand-held blender. Spread
spinach over base and place in oven for 10 minutes. Remove from oven.
Break an egg over the middle of each pizza and return to oven for 5 minutes.

spinach, escarole & swiss chard pizza

Prepare the basic recipe, using 225 g (8 oz) of an assorted fresh greens:
(spinach, escarole, and Swiss chard) in place of the spinach.

variations

garden vegetable pizza

see base recipe page 60

garden vegetable pizza with cauliflower
Prepare the basic recipe. Roast ½ head of cauliflower, broken into florets,
in 200°C (400°F / Gas Mark 6) oven for 25 to 30 minutes. Add roasted
cauliflower with other vegetables.

garden vegetable pizza with pesto
Prepare the basic recipe, replacing basic pizza sauce with 60 ml (4 tbsp)
pesto (page 26) per pizza.

garden vegetable pizza with herb base
Prepare the basic recipe, lightly glazing the edge of the pizza bases with
olive oil. Sprinkle each with 2.5 ml (½ tsp) Italian seasoning.

balsamic garden vegetable pizza
Prepare the basic recipe, tossing the vegetable slices in 30 ml (2 tbsp)
balsamic vinegar mixed with 60 ml (4 tbsp) olive oil before grilling them.

spring vegetable pizza
Prepare the basic recipe, omitting the aubergine and courgettes. Steam 8 to
12 thin asparagus spears per pizza until tender. Arrange on each pizza along
with 50 g (2 oz) sliced mushrooms and 2 to 4 marinated artichoke hearts,
drained and roughly chopped.

pesto pizza

see base recipe page 63

pesto & artichoke heart pizza

Prepare the basic recipe, adding 3 to 4 drained and roughly chopped marinated artichoke hearts to each pizza before adding the cheese. Replace mozzarella with 4 to 5 teaspoon-sized chunks of chèvre (goat's cheese) if desired.

pesto & sun-dried tomato pizza

Prepare the basic recipe, replacing fresh tomato slices with 3 to 4 drained and roughly chopped sun-dried tomatoes on each pizza.

pesto & roasted red pepper pizza

Prepare the basic recipe, adding 3 to 4 sections of roasted red pepper, drained and cut into strips, to each pizza before adding the cheese.

pesto & roasted aubergine pizza

Prepare the basic recipe, adding 3 to 4 slices diced roasted aubergine to each pizza, before adding the cheese.

pesto pizza with sesame base

Prepare the basic recipe, lightly glazing the edge of the base with olive oil and sprinkling with 2.5 ml (½ tsp) sesame seeds before adding the pesto and toppings.

variations

wild mushrooms on wholemeal base pizza

see base recipe page 64

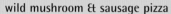

wild mushroom & sausage pizza
Prepare the basic recipe. Remove 450 g (1 lb) Italian sausage or herby sausage from its casings in small chunks and brown in 15–30 ml (1–2 tbsp) olive oil until cooked. Drain and divide between the 3 pizzas.

wild mushroom & sage pizza
Prepare the basic recipe, replacing the dried rosemary with 1.25 ml (¼ tsp) dried or 5 ml (1 tsp) chopped fresh sage.

wild mushroom & tapenade pizza
Prepare the basic recipe, adding 8 half-teaspoon dollops of tapenade (page 27) per pizza over the shredded mozzarella.

wild mushroom & crème fraiche pizza
Prepare the basic recipe, omitting the mozzarella and adding 30–45 ml (2–3 tsp) of crème fraiche over the mushroom mixture.

wild mushrooms with chèvre and parsley on basic base
Prepare the basic recipe, replacing the wholemeal base with the basic thin base recipe. Omit the mozzarella and add 3 to 4 teaspoons of chèvre to each pizza over the mushroom mixture. Once pizzas have baked, sprinkle each with 2.5 ml (½ tsp) chopped fresh flat-leaf parsley.

four seasons pizza

see base recipe page 66

spring pizza
Prepare the basic recipe, keeping only spring topping. Double the quantity of asparagus and chop into 2.5-cm (1-in) pieces. Add 900 g (2 lb) fresh leeks. Using only the white and pale green ends, clean and slice into matchstick-shaped pieces. Steam vegetables together, then toss in 45 ml (3 tbsp) vinaigrette. Spread ⅓ vegetable mixture over each pizza base.

summer pizza
Prepare the basic recipe, keeping only summer topping. Use 350 ml (12 fl oz) pesto and spread ⅓ over each pizza base. Garnish with fresh tomato slices if desired.

autumn pizza
Prepare the basic recipe, keeping only autumn topping. Use Use 350 ml (12 fl oz) red pepper hummus and spread ⅓ over each base. Add ½ sliced red pepper to each pizza before baking.

winter pizza
Prepare the basic recipe, keeping only winter topping. Use 675 g (1½ lb) ricotta cheese and 60 g (2½ oz) grated Parmesan, and season with nutmeg, salt and pepper to taste. Spread ⅓ of the ricotta mixture over each pizza. Add 3 to 4 drained and chopped artichoke hearts per pizza, if desired.

variations

pizza bianca

see base recipe page 67

four-cheese pizza bianca
Prepare the basic recipe, replacing the cheese quantities with 75 g (3 oz) grated mozzarella, 75 g (3 oz) grated Fontina, 45 ml (3 tbsp) grated Parmesan, and 25 g (1 oz) grated Pecorino Romano.

pizza bianca with black olives
Prepare the basic recipe, adding 50 g (2 oz) pitted black olive slices per pizza over the spinach mixture.

pizza bianca with shrimp
Prepare the basic recipe, adding 115 g (4 oz) peeled and cooked shrimp per pizza over the spinach mixture.

pizza bianca with rosemary
Prepare the basic recipe, replacing the basil with 5 ml (1 tsp) crumbled dried rosemary.

pizza bianca with sesame base
Prepare the basic recipe, lightly glazing the 1-cm (½-in) border with extra-virgin olive oil and sprinkling with 2.5 ml (½ tsp) sesame seeds per pizza.

variations

tapenade pizza

see base recipe page 69

tapenade pizza with roasted vegetables
Prepare the basic recipe, adding 75 g (3 oz) assorted roasted vegetables, such as red pepper, red onion, courgette and aubergine, per pizza, before adding the chèvre.

tapenade pizza with anchovies & red pepper
Prepare the basic recipe, adding 6 to 8 marinated anchovies, drained and patted dry, and ½ sliced red bell pepper per pizza before adding the chèvre.

tapenade pizza with bocconcini
Prepare the basic recipe, replacing the chèvre with an equal quantity of Bocconcini (small mozzarella balls).

tapenade pizza with feta & cherry tomatoes
Prepare the basic recipe, adding 6 to 8 cherry tomatoes per pizza. Slice tomatoes in half lengthways and arrange them over the tapenade. Replace the chèvre with an equal quantity of feta.

tapenade pizza with shiitake mushrooms
Prepare the basic recipe, adding 115 g (4 oz) shiitake mushroom caps per pizza. Slice mushroom in 1-cm (½-in) strips and arrange them over the tapenade.

smoked salmon & caper pizza

see base recipe page 70

smoked mackerel pizza

Prepare the basic recipe, replacing the smoked salmon with an equal quantity of smoked mackerel.

smoked trout pizza

Prepare the basic recipe, replacing the smoked salmon with an equal quantity of smoked trout.

smoked salmon & red onion pizza

Prepare the basic recipe, adding ½ thinly sliced red onion, divided between the 3 pizzas.

smoked salmon & caper pizza on wholemeal base

Prepare the basic recipe, replacing the basic thin pizza base with the wholemeal thin pizza base (page 23).

smoked salmon & fresh tomato pizza

Prepare the basic recipe, adding 1 thinly sliced fresh tomato, divided between the 3 pizzas.

fresh tomato pizza

see base recipe page 73

fresh tomato pizza with saint-agur

Prepare the basic recipe, adding 115 g (4 oz) crumbled Saint-Agur cheese
over the sauce on each pizza. Omit the mozzarella. Sprinkle each pizza
with 60 ml (4 tbsp) grated Parmesan before adding the chopped basil.

fresh tomato pizza with bocconcini

Prepare the basic recipe, replacing shredded mozzarella with 115 g (4 oz)
sliced bocconcini (small mozzarella balls) per pizza.

fresh tomato pizza with marinated artichoke hearts

Prepare the basic recipe, adding 3 to 4 marinated artichoke hearts, drained
and roughly chopped, per pizza. Place the artichoke pieces over the
mozzarella before baking.

fresh tomato pizza with pepperoni

Prepare the basic recipe, adding 6 to 8 slices of pepperoni per pizza.
Place pepperoni the slices over the mozzarella before baking.

fresh tomato pizza with oregano

Prepare the basic recipe, replacing the fresh basil leaves with 30 ml (2 tbsp)
fresh chopped oregano and the chopped basil with 30 ml (2 tbsp) fresh
chopped oregano.

variations

chèvre, rocket & pear pizza

see base recipe page 74

chèvre, rocket, pear & walnut pizza
Prepare the basic recipe, adding 30 ml (2 tbsp) chopped walnuts to each pizza, over the rocket leaves.

chèvre, rocket & olive pizza
Prepare the basic recipe, omitting the pear slices. Add 30 ml (2 tbsp) sliced black olives to each pizza before adding the rocket leaves.

chèvre, rocket & field mushroom pizza
Prepare the basic recipe, omitting the pear slices. Add 2 sliced field mushrooms to each pizza, over the chèvre mixture.

chèvre, rocket, pear & prosciutto pizza
Prepare the basic recipe, adding 2 to 4 slices prosciutto, torn into strips, per pizza over the pear slices.

chèvre, rocket & pear pizza with balsamic vinegar
Prepare the basic recipe. After baking, drizzle each pizza with 10 ml (2 tsp) balsamic vinegar.

rustic pizzas
& calzones

These hearty pizzas and calzones are pure comfort

food. Overflowing with luscious cheeses and cured

meats, they are the pizzas traditionally made by

home cooks throughout Italy.

artichoke heart & ricotta calzones

see variations page 104

Be sure to seal your calzones tightly, so that none of the delicious filling leaks out during baking!

1 recipe basic calzone dough (page 18)
225 g (8 oz) ricotta cheese
75 g (3 oz) 1-cm (¼–in) cubes mozzarella cheese
30 ml (2 tbsp) finely grated Parmesan cheese

75 g (3 oz) drained and roughly chopped marinated artichoke hearts
30 ml (2 tbsp) flat-leaf finely chopped parsley
freshly ground black pepper

Preheat the oven to 230°C (450°F / Gas Mark 8). While the dough is resting, prepare the filling. In a large bowl, combine the cheeses, artichoke hearts, and parsley. Add freshly ground black pepper to taste. Follow the instructions on page 18 for rolling out the dough into 4 equal discs. Using a pastry brush, glaze the top edge of each round with water. Spoon ¼ of the filling onto the lower half of each round. Fold the top over so that the edge of the top sits 1 cm (½ in) away from the bottom half. Lightly glaze the edge of the top piece and fold the bottom over to seal tightly. Make a 1-cm (½-in) slit in the top to allow steam to escape. Place the calzones on a pre-heated baking sheet lined with baking paper and bake on the middle rack for 15 to 20 minutes, or until the filling is hot and the base is golden brown.

Makes 4 calzones

rustic pancetta &
mortadella pizza

see variations page 105

This pizza features a spectacular blend of smoked cheeses and cured meats.

1 recipe basic double pizza
base (page 19)
1–2 mild Italian or herby
sausages, removed from
casings
115 g (4 oz) pancetta, cubed
15 ml (1 tbsp) extra-virgin
olive oil

115 g (4 oz) mortadella, cut
into small pieces
225 g (8 oz) ricotta cheese
50 g (2 oz) smoked provolone
cubes
50 g (2 oz) grated mozzarella
cheese
45 ml (3 tbsp) finely grated

Parmesan cheese
2 eggs, lightly beaten
1 garlic clove, minced
30 ml (2 tbsp) chopped flat-
leaf parsley
pinch crushed red pepper
flakes
freshly ground black pepper

Preheat the oven to 200°C (400°F / Gas Mark 6). While dough is in its second rising, make
the filling. Fry the crumbled sausage meat and pancetta cubes in olive oil for 5 to 6 minutes,
until sausage is cooked through (remove pancetta from pan earlier as soon as it is crisp).
Drain and place in large bowl. Add mortadella, cheeses, eggs, garlic and seasonings, and stir
until well combined. On a lightly floured surface, roll out first ball of dough to a 30-cm
(12-in) round. Add flour as necessary to prevent sticking. Place dough in a 23-cm (9-in)
springform pan, so there is 2.5 cm (1 in) hanging over the edge. Pour filling into pan. Roll
out second ball to a 23-cm (9-in) round and place over the filling. Fold the overhanging
dough from the bottom round over the edge of the top round, pinching lightly to seal. Make
1 to 2 slits in the top to allow steam to escape. Bake in middle of oven for 45 minutes. Leave
to stand for 10 to 15 minutes before slicing into 8 wedges.

Makes one 23-cm (9-in) double-crusted pizza. Serves 8.

rustic ricotta & salami pizza

see variations page 106

This is similar to the Pancetta & Mortadella Pizza, but with the peppery accent of salami.

1 recipe basic double pizza base (page 19)
225 g (8 oz) ricotta cheese
225 g (8 oz) dry salami, sliced and cut into
    quarters
1 fresh tomato, chopped

50 g (2 oz) smoked provolone cubes
50 g (2 oz) grated mozzarella cheese
45 ml (3 tbsp) finely grated Parmesan
30 ml (2 tbsp) chopped flat-leaf parsley
1 egg, lightly beaten

Preheat the oven to 200°C (400°F / Gas Mark 6). While the dough is in its second rising, make the filling.

Combine all ingredients in a bowl. Stir to blend evenly. Divide the dough into 2 balls, one slightly bigger than the other. On a lightly floured surface, roll out the first ball to a 30-cm (12-in) round. Add flour as necessary to prevent sticking. Place dough in a 23-cm (9-in) springform pan, so there is 2.5 cm (1 in) excess hanging over the edge. Pour the filling into pan.

Roll out the second ball of dough to a 23-cm (9-in) round and place over the filling. Fold the overhanging dough from the bottom round over the edge of the top round, pinching lightly to seal. Make 1 to 2 slits in the top to allow steam to escape.

Bake in the middle of the oven for 45 minutes. Leave to stand for 10 to 15 minutes before slicing into 8 wedges.

Makes one 9-in (23-cm) double-crusted pizza. Serves 8.

prawn panzerotti

see variations page 107

Prawns in a creamy sauce make this savoury turnover an indulgent treat.

1 recipe basic calzone dough (page 18)
675 g (1½ lb) prawn, cleaned and deveined
225 ml (8 fl oz) dry white wine
45 ml (3 tbsp) chopped flat-leaf parsley
2.5 ml (½ tsp) salt
60 g (2 ½ oz) unsalted butter

225 g (8 oz) sliced button mushrooms
2 large spring onions, chopped
45 ml (3 tbsp) all-purpose flour
120 ml (4 fl oz) single cream or creamy milk
45 ml (3 tbsp) grated Fontina cheese

Preheat oven to 230°C (450°F / Gas Mark 8). While the dough is resting, prepare the filling. In large saucepan, combine prawn, wine, and parsley. Add enough water to just cover the prawn. Bring to a boil and simmer for 5 to 6 minutes, until prawn are pink and opaque. Using a slotted spoon, remove prawns from liquid. Return liquid to boil. Cook until liquid has reduced to 1 cup. Strain and set aside.

Melt 25 g (1 oz) of the butter in saucepan. Sauté mushrooms and spring onions for 5 to 6 minutes, until mushrooms are tender. Set aside. Melt the remaining butter in a seperate saucepan. Add flour, and stir until the mixture forms a smooth paste and begins to bubble. Whisk in reserved wine liquid. Cook and stir for 1 minute. Add cream, prawns, mushrooms, and cheese. Stir until cheese has melted and mixture is heated evenly. Follow the instructions on page 18 for rolling out the dough into 4 equal rounds. Using a pastry brush, glaze the top edge of the circles with water. Spoon some filling onto the lower half of each round – do

not overstuff, or they will leak. If there is extra filling, it can be served with the cooked panzerotti as a sauce. Fold the top over so that the edge of the top sits 1 cm (½ in) away from the bottom half. Lightly glaze the edge of the top piece and fold the bottom over to seal tightly. Make a 1-cm (½-in) slit in the top to allow steam to escape. Place the calzones on a pre-heated baking sheet lined with baking paper and bake on the middle rack for 15 to 20 minutes, or until the filling is hot and the base is golden brown.

Makes 4 calzones

broccoli, asiago & pine nut calzones

see variations page 108

These delectable calzones offer a nutritious boost from the broccoli and pine nuts.

1 recipe basic calzone basedough (page 18)
florets from 2 broccoli stalks, steamed until
    tender (or one 275 g (10 oz) packet frozen
    broccoli florets, thawed and drained)
225 g (8 oz) ricotta cheese
50 g (2 oz) grated mozzarella cheese

45 ml (3 tbsp) finely grated Asiago cheese
40 g (1½ oz) pine nuts, toasted and roughly
    chopped
salt and freshly ground black pepper
pinch of grated nutmeg

Preheat oven to 230°C (450°F / Gas Mark 8). While the dough is resting, prepare the filling. Chop broccoli florets and combine with cheeses and pine nuts. Season with salt, pepper, and nutmeg.

Follow the instructions on page 18 for rolling out the dough into 4 equal circles. Using a pastry brush, glaze the top edge of the rounds with water. Spoon about 60 ml (4 tbsp) filling onto the lower half of each circle. Fold the top over so that the edge of the top sits 1 cm (½ in) away from the bottom half. Lightly glaze the edge of the top piece and fold the bottom over to seal tightly. Make a 1-cm (½-in) slit in the top to allow steam to escape.

Place the calzones on a preheated baking sheet lined with baking paper and bake on the middle rack for 15 to 20 minutes, or until the filling is hot and the crust is golden brown.

Makes 4 calzones.

mozzarella & ham stromboli

see variations page 109

A stromboli – a rolled pizza – is named for the volcanic island of Stromboli because of the way the cheese bubbles out of the base during baking.

1 recipe basic calzone dough (page 18)
450 g (1 lb) grated mozzarella
225 g (8 oz) ham, thinly sliced

30 ml (2 tbsp) unsalted butter, melted
30 ml (2 tbsp) finely grated Parmesan cheese

Preheat oven to 190°C (375°F / Gas Mark 5). Knock back the dough. Using a sharp knife, divide it into 2 equal pieces. Shape each into a ball and roll out into two 36-cm (14-in) x 30-cm (12-in) rectangles.

Spread half the grated mozzarella over the first rectangle, leaving a 1-cm (½-in) border. Top with a layer of half the ham slices. Starting from the long edge, roll tightly to form a long cylinder. Pinch seam to seal and fold ends under. Repeat process with the second ball of dough.

Brush each stromboli with 15 ml (1 tbsp) melted butter and sprinkle each with 15 ml (1 tbsp) grated Parmesan. Place the stromboli on a baking sheet lined with baking paper and bake on the middle rack for 20 to 25 minutes, or until the base is golden brown.

Transfer to a wire rack to cool for 5 minutes. Slice on the diagonal.

Makes 2 stromboli. Serves 6–8.

fontina & basil piadine

see variations page 110

Piadine are flatbreads that are baked quickly in a skillet and then folded over a simple filling. If you cannot find the authentic, semi-firm Fontina Valle d'Aosta, you can substitute the firm fontina found in most supermarkets, grated instead of crumbled.

400 g (14 oz) plain flour
5 ml (1 tsp) salt
2.5 ml (½ tsp) baking powder
225 ml (8 fl oz) warm water

60 ml (4 tbsp) extra-virgin olive oil
225 g (8 oz) crumbled Fontina Valle d'Aosta
16 fresh basil leaves, torn into pieces

To prepare the dough, combine flour, salt, and baking powder in the bowl of a standing mixer. Add water and oil. Using dough hook, run mixer on low speed for 1 to 2 minutes, or until dough is smooth and elastic. Turn dough onto lightly floured surface and knead by hand for another 1 to 2 minutes. Shape dough into ball and place in lightly oiled bowl. Cover with paper towel and set aside for 30 to 60 minutes. Using a sharp knife, cut dough into 8 equal pieces. Shape each piece into a ball; keep the remaining pieces covered. Using a rolling pin, roll out each ball to a 20 cm (8 in) round. Stack between sheets of baking paper.

Heat a nonstick skillet over medium-high heat. Place first piece of dough in skillet and cook for 30 seconds, until dough looks dry around the edges and is golden brown. Turn the piadina over and cook until second side is also golden brown. Remove piadina from pan, then fill with 1/8 of the Fontina and 2 torn fresh basil leaves. Repeat with remaining 7 rounds of dough.

Makes 8 piadine. Serves 8 as a light lunch or snack.

crab & parsley calzones

see variations page 111

The rich cream cheese and crab filling makes these calzones suitable for entertaining, but there is no reason not to enjoy them on a regular weeknight as well!

1 recipe basic calzone basedough (page 18)
115 g (4 oz) grated mozzarella
225 g (8 oz) cream cheese, softened
225 g (8 oz) crabmeat

4 large spring onions, finely chopped
1 garlic clove, finely chopped
30 ml (2 tbsp) finely chopped flat-leaf parsley

Preheat oven to 230°C (450°F / Gas Mark 8). Follow the instructions on page 18 for rolling the dough into 4 equal circles.

Combine the cheeses, crabmeat, spring onion, garlic, and parsley in a bowl until well blended. Using a pastry brush, glaze the top edge of each round with water. Spoon about 60 ml (4 tbsp) filling onto the lower half of each round.

Fold the top over so that the edge of the top sits 1 cm ($\frac{1}{2}$ in) away from the bottom half. Lightly glaze the edge of the top piece and fold the bottom over to seal tightly. Make a 1-cm ($\frac{1}{2}$-in) slit in the top to allow steam to escape.

Place the calzones on a pre-heated baking sheet lined with baking paper and bake on the middle rack for 15 to 20 minutes, or until the filling is hot and the crust is golden brown.

Makes 4 calzones.

cheddar & bacon stuffed pizza

see variations page 112

The stuffed pizza is a close relative of the Chicago deep-dish pizza, and this double-crust pizza has a distinctly American flavour!

1 recipe basic double pizza base (page 19)
225 g (8 oz) ricotta cheese
225 g (8 oz) bacon, fried until crisp and
    crumbled
50 g (2 oz) cheddar, cut into small cubes

25 g (1 oz) grated mozzarella
25 g (1 oz) grated Monterey Jack or extra
    cheddar
1 egg, lightly beaten

Preheat the oven to 200°C (400°F / Gas Mark 6). While the dough is in its second rising, make the filling.

Combine all ingredients in a bowl. Stir to blend evenly. Divide the dough into 2 balls, one slightly larger than the other. On a lightly floured surface, roll out first dough ball to a 30-cm (12-in) round. Add flour as necessary to prevent sticking.

Place dough in a 23-cm (9-in) springform pan, so there is 2.5 cm (1 in) hanging over the edge. Pour filling into pan. Roll out the second ball of dough to a 23-cm (9-in) round and place over the filling. Fold the overhanging dough from the bottom round over the edge of the top round, pinching lightly to seal. Make 1 to 2 slits in the top to allow steam to escape.

Bake in middle of oven for 45 minutes. Leave to stand for 10 to 15 minutes before slicing into 8 wedges.

Makes one 23-cm (9-in) stuffed pizza. Serves 8.

sausage & mushroom calzones

see variations page 113

With its combination of spicy and earthy flavours, this calzone is pure comfort food on a winter's evening.

1 recipe basic calzone basedough (page 18)
350 g (12 oz) Italian or herby sausage, removed
    from casings and crumbled
115 g (4 oz) sliced mushrooms
15 ml (1 tbsp) extra-virgin olive oil

½ recipe basic pizza sauce (page 25)
115 g (4 oz) shredded mozzarella
30 ml (2 tbsp) melted unsalted butter
20 ml (4 tsp) finely grated Parmesan

Preheat oven to 230°C (450°F / Gas Mark 8). While the dough is resting, prepare the filling. Brown the crumbled sausage meat and mushroom slices in olive oil for 5 to 6 minutes, until sausage is cooked through. Add the pizza sauce.

Follow the instructions on page 18 for rolling the dough into 4 equal circles. Using a pastry brush, glaze the top edge of the rounds with water. Spoon ¼ of the filling onto the lower half of each round. Sprinkle with 1/4 of the mozzarella. Fold the top over so that the edge of the top sits 1 cm (½ in) away from the bottom half. Lightly glaze the edge of the top piece and fold the bottom over to seal tightly. Make a 1-cm (½-in) slit in the top to allow steam to escape. Brush tops with melted butter and sprinkle with 5 ml (1 tsp) Parmesan cheese. Place the calzones on a pre-heated baking sheet lined with baking paper and bake on the middle rack for 15 to 20 minutes, or until the filling is hot and the crust is golden brown.

Makes 4 calzones.

variations

artichoke heart & ricotta calzone

see base recipe page 87

artichoke heart calzones with four cheeses

Prepare the basic recipe, reducing amount of cubed mozzarella cheese to 25 g (1 oz) and adding 25 g (1 oz) cubed fontina in its place.

artichoke heart & ricotta calzones with pancetta

Prepare the basic recipe, adding 100 g (3 ½ oz) cubed and fried pancetta to the filling mixture.

artichoke heart calzones with garlic and pepper

Prepare the basic recipe, adding 1 crushed garlic clove and a pinch of crushed red pepper flakes to the filling mixture.

artichoke heart calzones with basil

Prepare the basic recipe, replacing the flat-leaf parsley with an equal quantity of fresh basil.

artichoke heart calzones with white clams

Prepare the basic recipe, adding 115 g (4 oz) of cooked and shelled white clams to the filling mixture.

variations

rustic pancetta & mortadella pizza

see base recipe page 88

rustic parma ham & mortadella pizza
Prepare the basic recipe, replacing the pancetta with an equal quantity
of Parma ham, cut into small pieces.

rustic prosciutto & mortadella pizza
Prepare the basic recipe, replacing the pancetta with an equal
quantity of prosciutto, cut into small pieces.

rustic italian sausage pizza
Prepare the basic recipe, replacing the pancetta with 1 to 2 more sausages.

rustic pancetta & mortadella pizza with garlic & peppers
Prepare the basic recipe, sautéing ½ diced red bell pepper with the sausage
and pancetta. Add 1 additional finely chopped clove of garlic to the filling.

rustic pancetta & five-cheese pizza
Prepare the basic recipe, adding 25 g (1 oz) grated Romano Pecorino cheese
to the filling.

variations

rustic ricotta & salami pizza

see base recipe page 91

rustic ricotta & ground beef pizza

Prepare the basic recipe, replacing the salami with 225 g (8 oz) browned and drained lean beef.

rustic ricotta & merguez pizza

Prepare the basic recipe, replacing the salami with 225 g (8 oz) Merguez sausage, which has been removed from its casings, crumbled, browned and drained.

rustic ricotta & roast vegetable pizza

Prepare the basic recipe, replacing the salami with 250 g (9 oz) assorted roasted vegetable chunks.

rustic ricotta & spinach pizza

Prepare the basic recipe, replacing the salami with 450 g (1 lb) steamed baby spinach leaves. Add 1 minced clove garlic to the filling.

rustic ricotta & quinoa pizza

Prepare the basic recipe, replacing the salami with 150 g (5 oz) cooked quinoa. Replace flat-leaf parsley with equal quantity of corinander, and add 1 to 2 chopped spring onions to the filling.

prawn panzerotti

see base recipe page 92

prawn & basil panzerotti

Prepare the basic recipe, adding 30 ml (2 tbsp) chopped fresh basil to the filling.

prawn & asparagus panzerotti

Prepare the basic recipe, adding 3 to 4 asparagus spears, steamed and chopped to the filling.

prawn & crab panzerotti

Prepare the basic recipe, replacing half the amount of prawn with an equal quantity of crabmeat.

prawn & scallop panzerotti

Prepare the basic recipe, replacing half the amount of prawn with an equal quantity of small sautéed scallops.

prawn & clam panzerotti

Prepare the basic recipe, replacing half the amount of prawn with an equal quantity of cooked clams.

variations

broccoli, asiago & pine nut calzones

see base recipe page 95

broccoli, parmesan & pine nut calzones
Prepare the basic recipe, replacing the Asiago with an equal quantity
of Parmesan.

spinach, asiago & pine nut calzones
Prepare the basic recipe, replacing the broccoli with 450 g (1 lb) cleaned,
stemmed, wilted, drained, and chopped spinach.

broccoli, asiago & garlic calzones
Prepare the basic recipe, omitting the pine nuts and adding
1 crushed garlic clove.

broccoli & sun-dried tomato calzones
Prepare the basic recipe, omitting the pine nuts and adding
2 to 3 drained and chopped sun-dried tomatoes to the filling.

broccoli & mushroom calzones
Prepare the basic recipe, replacing the pine nuts with 115 g (4 oz) sliced
button mushrooms that have been sautéed in 15 g (½ oz) butter
for 4 to 5 minutes to the filling.

mozzarella & ham stromboli

see base recipe page 96

mozzarella & basil pesto stromboli
Prepare the basic recipe, omitting ham slices. Spread each rectangle with 1/4 of the basil pesto (page 26). Replace mozzarella with 450 g (1 lb) bocconcini (small mozzarella balls) torn into pieces and scattered over the pesto.

mozzarella & pepperoni stromboli
Prepare the basic recipe, replacing the deli ham with an equal quantity of pepperoni.

three-cheese stromboli
Prepare the basic recipe, substituting 50 g (2 oz) grated provolone and 50 g (2 oz) grated fontina for 225 g (8 oz) of the grated mozzarella.

mozzarella & garlic stromboli
Prepare the basic recipe, spreading each rectangle of dough with 30 ml (2 tbsp) roasted garlic purée before adding the cheese and ham.

mozzarella & tomato stromboli
Prepare the basic recipe, adding 1 thinly sliced fresh tomato to each stromboli before rolling it up.

variations

fontina & basil piadine

see base recipe page 98

fontina, broccoli & basil piadine
Prepare the basic recipe, adding 350 g (12 oz) of steamed and chopped broccoli florets to the filling.

fontina, tomato & basil piadine
Prepare the basic recipe, adding 1 to 2 tomato slices per piadina to the filling.

monterey jack & three-pepper piadine
Prepare the basic recipe, replacing the Fontina with an equal quantity of grated Monterey Jack or Red Leicester cheese. Omit basil and season each piadina with freshly ground mixed peppercorns (black, white and pink/red peppercorns).

fontina, ham & basil piadine
Prepare the basic recipe, adding 1 to 2 pieces of sliced cooked ham per piadina.

fontina & spinach piadine with nutmeg
Prepare the basic recipe, omitting the basil. Add several leaves of fresh baby spinach and a pinch of nutmeg to each piadina.

variations

crab & parsley calzones

see base recipe page 99

crab & chive calzones
Prepare the basic recipe, replacing the parsley with 30 ml (2 tbsp) freshly chopped chives.

crab & sweetcorn calzones
Prepare the basic recipe, adding 75 g (3 oz) ½ cup frozen corn to the filling mixture.

scallop & crab calzones
Prepare the basic recipe, using only 115 g (4 oz) crabmeat and adding 12 cooked small scallops to the filling.

crab & thai basil calzones
Prepare the basic recipe, replacing the parsley with 30 ml (2 tbsp) freshly chopped Thai basil.

crab & mussel calzones
Prepare the basic recipe, using only 175 g (6 oz) crabmeat and 12 cooked small mussels.

cheddar & bacon stuffed pizza

see base recipe page 101

cheddar & bacon stuffed pizza with herb base
Prepare the basic recipe, adding 5 ml (1 tsp) Italian seasoning to the flour mixture when making the dough.

havarti & parma ham stuffed pizza
Prepare the basic recipe, replacing the cheddar and Monterey Jack with 115 g (4 oz) grated Havarti cheese, and replacing the bacon with an equal quantity of Parma ham, torn into strips.

cheddar, bacon & tomato stuffed pizza
Prepare the basic recipe, adding 1 chopped fresh tomato to the filling mixture.

cheddar, bacon & pea stuffed pizza
Prepare the basic recipe, adding 60 g (2½ oz) frozen green peas to the filling mixture.

provolone & pancetta stuffed pizza
Prepare the basic recipe, replacing the cheddar and the Monterey Jack with 115 g (4 oz) grated Provolone, and the bacon with an equal quantity of fried pancetta, cubes.

variations

sausage & mushroom calzones

see base recipe page 102

sausage, mushroom & pepper calzones
Prepare the basic recipe, adding 1 seeded and sliced green pepper
to the sausage and mushrooms.

sausage, mushroom & boursin calzones
Prepare the basic recipe, replacing the mozzarella with 225 g (8 oz)
Boursin (soft unripened cheese). Place 50 g (2 oz) Boursin in teaspoonfuls
over the filling before sealing the calzones.

sausage, mushroom & sun-dried tomato calzones
Prepare the basic recipe, adding 2 large roughly chopped sun-dried
tomatoes to the filling mixture with the pizza sauce.

turkey pepperoni & mushroom calzones
Prepare the basic recipe, omitting the sausage. Place 3 to 4 slices of turkey
pepperoni or smoked turkey over the dough before adding the mushrooms
and sauce.

smoked tofu & mushroom calzones
Prepare the basic recipe, replacing the sausage with an equal quantity
of crumbled smoked tofu.

international pizzas

Wherever pizza is popular, people have experimented with new toppings. Using local ingredients and taste preferences as inspiration, many regions have developed their own specialty toppings. In some cases, as with the Hawaiian or Parisian pizzas, the name evolved in an entirely different location, where a recipe was developed to evoke the flavours associated with that distant place.

hawaiian pizza

see variations page 132

This pizza, made famous by its ham and pineapple topping, is especially popular with children.

1 recipe basic Neapolitan pizza base (page 20)
1 recipe basic pizza sauce (page 25)
350 g (12 oz) shredded mozzarella

200 g (7 oz) pineapple pieces, drained and
    patted dry
150 g (5 oz) diced cooked ham

Following the instructions on page 15, preheat a pizza stone in an oven at the maximum setting, usually 240°C (475°F / Gas Mark 9) and roll out two 30-cm (12-in) circles of dough.

Lightly dust pizza peel with flour or cornmeal. Place one disc of pizza dough on peel and spread with half the pizza sauce, leaving a 1-cm (½-in) border.

Sprinkle with 175 g (6 oz) grated mozzarella and top with half the pineapple pieces and half the ham. Gently shake the pizza from the peel to the stone.

Bake 4 to 6 minutes, until cheese is melting and base is puffy around the edges and crisp on the bottom. Slide the peel back under the pizza to remove from oven. Repeat with the other pizza.

Makes two 30-cm (12-in) pizzas. Serves 6–8.

greek pizza

see variations page 133

Every bite of this pizza bursts with the classic flavors associated with Greece — feta, olives and tomato.

1 recipe basic Neapolitan pizza base (page 20)
15 ml (1 tbsp) extra-virgin olive oil
1 small red onion, thinly sliced
1 garlic clove, finely chopped

3 large fresh tomatoes, sliced
10 ml (2 tsp) dried oregano, crumbled
50 g (2 oz) pitted black olives, sliced
350 g (12 oz) crumbled feta cheese

Following the instructions on page 15, preheat a pizza stone in an oven at the maximum setting, usually 240°C (475°F / Gas Mark 9) and roll out two 30-cm (12-in) rounds of dough.

To prepare the toppings, heat olive oil in a frying pan. Add onion and garlic. Cook for 2 to 3 minutes, until onion softens.

Lightly dust a pizza peel with flour or cornmeal. Place one pizza dough round on peel and spread with half the onion mixture, leaving a 1-cm (1/2-in) border. Arrange half the tomato slices over the onions and sprinkle with 5 ml (1 tsp) oregano. Scatter half the olives and half the crumbled feta on top. Gently shake pizza from the peel to the stone.

Bake 4 to 6 minutes, until cheese is melting and base is puffy around edges and crisp on the bottom. Slide the peel back under the pizza to remove from oven. Repeat with the other pizza.

Makes two 30-cm (12-in) pizzas. Serves 6–8.

parisian pizza

see variations page 134

With shrimps, fresh mushrooms, and sun-dried tomatoes, this pizza has a delightful medley of flavours and textures.

1 recipe basic Neapolitan pizza base (page 20)
1 recipe basic pizza sauce (page 25)
350 g (12 oz) shredded mozzarella
450 g (1 lb) cooked shelled shrimps

115 g (4 oz) sliced white mushrooms
6–8 sun-dried tomatoes in oil, drained
    and coarsely chopped

Following the instructions on page 15, preheat a pizza stone in an oven at the maximum setting, usually 240°C (475°F / Gas Mark 9) and roll out two 30-cm (12-in) circles of dough.

Lightly dust a pizza peel with flour or cornmeal. Place one dough round on the peel and spread with half the pizza sauce.

Top with half the mozzarella, and distribute half the shrimps, mushrooms and sun-dried tomatoes over the cheese. Gently shake the pizza from the peel to the stone.

Bake for 4 to 6 minutes, until cheese is melting and base is puffy around edges and crisp on the bottom.

Slide the peel back under the pizza to remove from oven. Repeat with the other pizza.

Makes two 30-cm (12-in) pizzas. Serves 6–8.

brooklyn gourmet pizza

see variations page 135

The authentic Brooklyn Gourmet Pizza is baked in a brick oven and sliced into pieces that are big enough to fold in half. This is as close as you can get at home!

1 recipe basic Neapolitan pizza base (page 20)
175 g (6 oz) low fat mozzarella, thinly sliced
175 g (6 oz) full fat mozzarella, thinly sliced
5 ml (1 tsp) dried oregano, crumbled
freshly ground black pepper

225 g (8 oz) canned chopped tomatoes, drained
and crushed
45 ml (3 tbsp) extra-virgin olive oil
2.5 ml (½ tsp) dried basil, or 6–8 fresh basil
leaves, torn

Following the instructions on page 15, preheat a pizza stone in an oven at the maximum setting, usually 240°C (475°F / Gas Mark 9) and roll out two 30-cm (12-in) rounds of dough.

Lightly dust pizza peel with flour or cornmeal. Place one dough round on peel and place half the mozzarella slices over the dough, using a mixture of full fat and low fat mozzarellas. Sprinkle with black pepper and oregano. Arrange half the crushed tomatoes over the seasonings, leaving spaces between tomato pieces. Drizzle with 20 ml (4 tbsp) olive oil. Gently shake pizza from the peel onto the stone.

Bake for 4 to 6 minutes, until cheese is melting and base is puffy around edges and crisp on the bottom. Slide the peel back under the pizza to remove from the oven. Sprinkle with half of the basil. Repeat with the other pizza.

Makes two 30-cm (12-in) pizzas. Serves 6–8.

turkish pizza

see variations page 136

Inspired by the Turkish dish called Lahmacun, this pizza has the same luxurious ingredients – lamb scented with cinnamon, allspice, and cloves; tomatoes; and toasted pine nuts. The only real difference is this one is eaten flat instead of rolled or folded.

1 recipe basic Turkish pizza dough (page 15)
15 ml (1 tbsp) oil
1/2 red onion, finely chopped
450 g (1 lb) minced lamb
225 g (8 oz) drained canned whole tomatoes
30 ml (2 tbsp) tomato puree
60 ml (4 tbsp) finely chopped flat-leaf parsley
45 ml (3 tbsp) pine nuts, toasted

1.25 ml (¼ tsp) ground cinnamon
⅛ tsp minced allspice
generous pinch of minced cloves
pinch of crushed red pepper flakes
2.5 ml (½ tsp) salt
2.5 m.l (½ tsp) freshly ground black pepper
15 ml (1 tbsp) fresh lemon juice
110 g (4 oz) unsalted butter, melted

Following the instructions on page 15, let pizza dough rise while you make the lamb topping. To prepare the topping, heat the 15 ml (1 tbsp) oil in large frying pan. Add finely chopped onion and cook for 2 minutes, until translucent. Add lamb and cook until browned through. Stir in tomatoes, tomato puree, parsley, pine nuts and seasonings. Simmer for 10 to 15 minutes, then add lemon juice. Preheat a baking stone in an oven at 230°C (450°F / Gas Mark 8). Using a sharp knife, divide the dough into 16 egg-sized balls. Using rolling pin or fingers, stretch out each ball to form a 15-cm (6-in) round which is 3 mm (⅛ in) thick. Place on a lightly oiled baking sheet and set aside for 10 minutes. Top each one with 30 ml (2 tbsp) lamb mixture and drizzle the remaining butter over them. Place Turkish pizzas on baking stone and bake for 8 to 10 minutes, until the edges of the pizzas are golden.

Makes 16 small pizzas. Serves 6–8.

montreal pizza

see variations page 137

Montreal is famous for its smoked meat, so it wasn't long before someone thought of putting it on pizza.

1 recipe basic Neapolitan pizza base (page 20)
1 recipe basic pizza sauce (page 25)
350 g (12 oz) grated mozzarella cheese
100 g (3½ oz) Montreal smoked meat, sliced
    and cut into 2.5-cm (1-in) pieces

Following the instructions on page 15, preheat a pizza stone in an oven at the maximum setting, usually 240°C (475°F / Gas Mark 9) and roll out two 30-cm (12-in) rounds of dough.

Lightly dust pizza peel with flour or cornmeal. Place pizza dough round on the peel and spread with half the pizza sauce.

Sprinkle with 175 g (6 oz) grated mozzarella and arrange half the smoked meat pieces over the cheese. Gently shake the pizza from the peel to the stone.

Bake for 5 to 7 minutes, until the cheese is melting and base is puffy around the edges and crisp on the bottom. Slide the peel back under the pizza to remove from the oven. Repeat with the other pizza.

Makes two 30-cm (12-in) pizzas. Serves 6–8.

louisiana pizza

see variations page 138

With pieces of tender chicken, sweet corn kernels and a chive and ricotta topping, this original pizza is extremely satisfying.

1 recipe basic Neapolitan pizza base (page 20)
15 g (1 tbsp) unsalted butter
1 red pepper, diced
1 green bell pepper, diced
75 g (3 oz) frozen or canned sweet corn kernels

1 diced cooked chicken breast
salt and freshly ground black pepper
115 g (4 oz) ricotta cheese
30 ml (2 tbsp) finely chopped fresh chives
1 recipe basic pizza sauce (page 25)

Following the instructions on page 15, preheat a pizza stone in an oven at the maximum setting, usually 240°C (475°F / Gas Mark 9) and roll out two 30-cm (12-in) rounds of dough.

To prepare the topping, melt the butter over medium heat in large saucepan. Add diced peppers and cook for 1 to 2 minutes until they begin to soften. Remove from heat and stir in corn and chicken. Season to taste. In small bowl, combine ricotta and chives. Lightly dust a pizza peel with flour or cornmeal. Place one pizza dough round on peel and spread with half the pizza sauce. Spread half the chicken and corn mixture over the sauce and top with half the ricotta mixture. Gently shake the pizza from the peel onto the stone.

Bake 5 to 7 minutes, until the cheese is melting and base is puffy around edges and crisp on the bottom. Slide the peel back under the pizza to remove from the oven. Repeat with the other pizza.

Makes two 30-cm (12-in) pizzas. Serves 6–8.

mexican pizza

see variations page 139

This spicy pizza will warm things up on a cool evening!

1 recipe basic Neapolitan pizza base (page 20)
1 recipe basic pizza sauce (page 25)
350 g (12 oz) shredded mozzarella
225 g (8 oz) spicy sausage, cooked, halved and
    sliced into half-moon pieces
225 g (8 oz) pepperoni

½ mild onion, thinly sliced
1 small green pepper, seeded and
    thinly sliced
1–2 hot chillies, seeded and finely chopped
1 fresh tomato, sliced

Following the instructions on page 15, preheat a pizza stone in an oven at the maximum setting, usually 240°C (475°F / Gas Mark 9) and roll out two 30-cm (12-in) rounds of dough.

Lightly dust pizza peel with flour or cornmeal. Place one dough round on the peel and spread with half the pizza sauce.

Sprinkle with half the mozzarella and arrange half the sausage, pepperoni, onion, peppers, and tomato slices on top. Gently shake the pizza from the peel to the stone.

Bake for 5 to 7 minutes, until the cheese is melting and base is puffy around edges and crisp on the bottom. Slide the peel back under the pizza to remove from the oven. Repeat with the other pizza.

Makes two 30-cm (12-in) pizzas. Serves 6–8.

chicago deep-dish pizza

see variations page 140

The first deep-dish pizza is said to have been created at Chicago's Uno restaurant in the 1940s. Since then it has become something of a phenomenon.

1/3 recipe basic Chicago deep-dish pizza base
  (page 22)
175 g (6 oz) mozzarella cheese, sliced
450 g (1 lb) cannned Italian plum tomatoes,
  drained and broken into chunks with
  wooden spoon

2 cloves garlic, finely chopped
2.5 ml (1/2 tsp) dried basil
2.5 ml (1/2 tsp) dried oregano
salt and freshly ground black pepper
45 ml (3 tbsp) finely grated Parmesan cheese
15-30 ml (1–2 tbsp) extra-virgin olive oil

Following the instructions on page 15, roll the pizza dough into a ball.

Preheat oven to 240°C (470°F / Gas Mark 9). Lightly dust the dough ball with flour and using rolling pin, roll until disc is 27 cm (11 in) in diameter and 3 mm. (1/8 in) thick. Lightly oil a 23-cm (9-in) cake pan that is 5 cm (2 in) deep. Fit the dough in the pan so that the edges are flush with the edge of the pan.

Arrange the mozzarella slices in a single layer over the bottom of the dough round. Place tomatoes over the cheese and sprinkle garlic and seasonings over tomatoes. Cover with grated Parmesan and drizzle oil in a clockwise circle over the top.

Bake for 35 to 40 minutes, until the filling is hot and the crust is puffy and golden brown.

Makes one 23-cm (9-in) deep-dish pizza. Serves 3–4

neapolitan pizza

see variations page 141

If you prepare the dough by hand and use San Marzano tomatoes for your sauce, your pizza will be as authentic as it can be without baking it in a wood-burning oven!

1 recipe basic Neapolitan pizza base (page 20)
1 recipe basic pizza sauce, made with San
    Marzano tomatoes (page 25)

2 garlic cloves, thinly sliced
pinch of dried oregano
30 ml (2 tbsp) extra-virgin olive oil

Following the instructions on page 15, preheat a pizza stone in an oven at the maximum setting, usually 240°C (475°F / Gas Mark 9) and roll out two 30-cm (12-in) circles of dough.

Lightly dust a pizza peel with flour. Place one dough round on the peel and spread with half the pizza sauce.

Arrange half the garlic slices over sauce and sprinkle with half the oregano.

Drizzle 15 ml (1 tbsp) olive oil in a clockwise motion over the top of the pizza. Gently shake the pizza from the peel onto the stone.

Bake for 4 to 6 minutes, until the crust is puffy around edges and crisp on the bottom. Slide the peel back under the pizza to remove from the oven. Repeat with the other pizza.

Makes two 30-cm (12-in) pizzas. Serves 6–8.

variations

hawaiian pizza

see base recipe page 115

hawaiian pizza on wholemeal base
Prepare the basic recipe, replacing 125 g (4½ oz) bread flour with 115 g
(4 oz) wholemeal flour.

hawaiian pizza with parma ham
Prepare the basic recipe, replacing the cooked ham with an equal quantity
of Parma ham, thinly sliced and torn into strips.

hawaiian pizza with prosciutto
Prepare the basic recipe, replacing the cooked ham with an equal
quantity of prosciutto, thinly sliced and torn into strips.

hawaiian pizza with figs
Prepare the basic recipe, adding 1 or 2 sliced fresh figs per pizza with
the pineapple pieces.

hawaiian pizza with grapes
Prepare the basic recipe, adding about 30 ml (2 tbsp) halved red grapes per
pizza with the pineapple pieces.

greek pizza

see base recipe page 116

greek pizza with marinated tofu

Prepare the basic recipe, adding 50 g (2 oz) marinated tofu cubes to each pizza with the olives and feta.

greek pizza with tzatziki

Prepare the basic recipe, spreading each pizza base with 30-45 ml (2-3 tbsp) prepared tzatziki before adding the onions and other toppings.

greek pizza with kalamata olives

Prepare the basic recipe, replacing the black olives with an equal quantity of sliced kalamata olives.

greek pizza on gluten-free base

Prepare the basic recipe, replacing the basic pan pizza base with the Gluten-Free Pizza Base (page 24).

greek pizza with lamb

Prepare the basic recipe, adding 225 g (8 oz) minced lamb to the onion mixture. Cook until lamb is browned and cooked through.

variations

parisian pizza

see base recipe page 119

parisian pizza with brie
Prepare the basic recipe, replacing the mozzarella with 225 g (8 oz) sliced Brie, divided between the pizzas.

parisian pizza with escargots
Prepare the basic recipe, adding 275 g (10 oz) small French escargots per pizza. To prepare the snails, sauté in 40 g (1½ oz) unsalted butter with 2 finely chopped garlic cloves and season with salt and freshly ground black pepper.

parisian pizza with camembert
Prepare the basic recipe, replacing the mozzarella with 225g (8 oz) sliced Camembert, divided between the pizzas.

parisian pizza with cocktail tomatoes
Prepare the basic recipe, adding 6 to 8 halved cocktail tomatoes per pizza, arranged over the cheese with the shrimp and mushrooms.

parisian pizza with rocket
Prepare the basic recipe, adding 115 g (4 oz) baby rocket leaves to each pizza, arranged over the cheese with the shrimps and mushrooms.

brooklyn gourmet pizza

see base recipe page 120

brooklyn gourmet sausage pizza
Prepare the recipe, replacing tomatoes with basic sausage pizza sauce (page 28).

brooklyn gourmet meat lovers' pizza
Prepare the basic recipe, adding 175 g (6 oz) sliced pepperoni and 225 g (8 oz) Italian or herby pork sausage (cooked, halved and sliced into half-moon pieces), divided between both pizzas over the cheese.

brooklyn gourmet vegetarian pizza
Prepare the basic recipe, adding 115 g (4 oz) sliced mushrooms, 4 to 6 drained and roughly chopped sun-dried tomatoes, ½ thinly sliced mild onion, and 50 g (2 oz) sliced pitted black olives, divided between both pizzas over the tomatoes.

brooklyn gourmet pizza with ratatouille
Prepare the basic recipe, replacing tomatoes with 1 recipe ratatouille (page 29).

brooklyn gourmet salmon pizza
Prepare the basic recipe, omitting the crushed tomatoes and mozzarella. Blend 60 ml (4 tbsp) pesto (page 26) with 250 g (8 oz) ricotta. Spread mixture over bases and bake according to instructions. Remove from oven and top each pizza with 75 g (3 oz) smoked salmon, sliced thinly, and cut into strips.

variations

turkish pizza

see base recipe page 123

turkish pizza with spiced minced beef
Prepare the basic recipe, replacing minced lamb with an equal quantity
of lean minced beef.

turkish pizza with spiced minced pork
Prepare the basic recipe, replacing minced lamb with an equal
quantity of minced pork.

turkish pizza with spiced minced turkey
Prepare the basic recipe, replacing minced lamb with an equal quantity
of minced turkey.

turkish pizza with crumbled feta
Prepare the basic recipe, topping each pizza with 15 ml (1 tbsp)
crumbled feta once they have been removed from the oven.

turkish pizza with spiced crumbled seitan
Prepare the basic recipe, replacing the minced lamb with an equal quantity
of crumbled seitan (wheat gluten meat substitute).

variations

montreal pizza

see base recipe page 124

montreal pizza with hot peppers
Prepare the basic recipe, adding 50 g (2 oz) sliced marinated hot peppers
to each pizza with the smoked meat.

montreal pizza with rye base
Prepare the basic recipe, replacing 50 g (2 oz) plain flour in the pizza dough
with 50 g (2 oz) rye flour.

montreal pizza with pastrami
Prepare the basic recipe, replacing the smoked meat with an equal quantity
of pastrami.

montreal pizza with corned beef
Prepare the basic recipe, replacing the smoked meat with an equal quantity
of corned beef.

montreal pizza with mustard
Prepare the basic recipe, dotting each piece of smoked meat with
Dijon or hot mustard.

variations

louisiana pizza

see base recipe page 127

louisiana cheese & corn pizza
Prepare the basic recipe, omitting chicken.

louisiana pizza with gumbo
Prepare the basic recipe, replacing basic pizza sauce with an equal quantity of store-bought gumbo. Omit chicken mixture. Top gumbo with ricotta mixture.

louisiana pizza with okra
Prepare the basic recipe, adding 225 g (8 oz) drained and sliced canned okra to the chicken and corn mixture.

louisiana pizza with lobster
Prepare the basic recipe, replacing the chicken with an equal quantity of cooked lobster pieces.

louisiana pizza with button mushrooms
Prepare the basic recipe, adding 225 g (8 oz) diced button mushrooms to the peppers.

variations

mexican pizza

see base recipe page 128

mexican pizza on tortilla
Prepare the basic recipe, replacing the Neapolitan base with 4 large store-bought or homemade tortillas (page 223). Divide sauce, cheese, and toppings in fourths and proceed with recipe.

tex-mex pizza
Prepare the basic recipe, replacing half the mozzarella with Monterey Jack cheese, if available or Cheddar cheese.

mexican pizza with cilantro
Prepare the basic recipe, adding 30 ml (2 tbsp) chopped fresh coriander to each pizza once it hs been removed from the oven.

mexican pizza with green salsa
Prepare the basic recipe, replacing the basic pizza sauce with 120 ml (4 fl oz) prepared green salsa per pizza.

mexican pizza with refried beans
Prepare the basic recipe, adding 115 g (4 oz) refried beans per pizza.

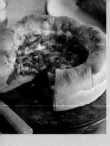

variations

chicago deep-dish pizza

see base recipe page 130

vegetable deep-dish pizza

Prepare the basic recipe, arranging thin slices of ½ mild onion, 115 g (4 oz) button mushrooms, and ½ sliced green pepper over cheese before adding crushed tomatoes.

sausage deep-dish pizza

Prepare the basic recipe, replacing ½ the crushed tomatoes with ½ recipe basic sausage pizza sauce (page 28).

four-cheese deep-dish pizza

Prepare the basic recipe, replacing half the mozzarella with 75 g (3 oz) sliced provolone. Add 25 g (1 oz) grated fontina to top of pizza before adding Parmesan.

spinach deep-dish pizza

Prepare the basic recipe, replacing crushed tomatoes and seasonings with 450 g (1 lb) spinach, rinsed, stemmed, squeeze dried and chopped. Sauté 225 g (8 oz) sliced mushrooms in 30 ml (2 tbsp) extra-virgin olive oil. When mushrooms are beginning to brown, add 2 cloves finely chopped garlic and cook for 2 minutes. Remove from heat, combine spinach and mushroom mixture. Season with salt and pepper. Proceed with recipe, or add 115 g (4 oz) sliced mozzarella over the spinach mixture before sprinkling with Parmesan.

variations

neapolitan pizza

see base recipe page 131

neapolitan pizza with anchovies
Prepare the basic recipe, adding 4 to 6 drained canned anchovy fillets per pizza. Arrange them like spokes from the centre of the pizza to the rim.

neapolitan pizza with ricotta
Prepare the basic recipe, adding 20-25 ml (4-5 tsp) ricotta cheese in dollops over the sauce.

neapolitan pizza with sardines
Prepare the basic recipe, adding 4 to 6 drained canned sardine fillets per pizza. Arrange them like spokes from the centre of the pizza to the rim.

neapolitan pizza with fresh basil
Prepare the basic recipe, adding 3 to 4 torn fresh basil leaves, per pizza. Scatter them over the sauce.

neapolitan pizza with herb crust
Prepare the basic recipe, adding 1.25 ml (¼ tsp) Italian seasoning to the basic Neapolitan pizza base recipe with the flour.

fougasse, focaccia & european flatbreads

These irresistible and versatile flatbreads from all corners of Europe make delicious sandwiches, picnic foods, or accompaniments for hearty soups and stews. Try the crisp flatbreads with dips and cheese; enjoy the oatcakes and barley bread with butter and jam for breakfast.

classic fougasse

see variations page 160

Dotted with plump black olives, this fragrant flatbread is hard to resist.

5 ml (1 tsp) active dried yeast
350 ml (12 fl oz) warm water
450 g (1 lb) plain flour
30 ml (2 tbsp) extra-virgin olive oil
10 ml (2 tsp) salt

175 g (6 oz) pitted black olives
25 g (1 oz) buckwheat flour
250 g (9 oz) wholemeal pastry flour, preferably
    fine milled

Sprinkle yeast over warm water in large bowl of standing mixer. Add 275 g (10 oz) cups plain flour and mix on slow speed for 1 minute. Cover bowl with cling film and set aside for 30 minutes. Add olive oil, salt, olives, and buckwheat flour to yeast mixture and stir to combine. Mix in wholemeal pastry flour. Add remaining plain flour and switch to dough hook attachment. Knead for 4 to 5 minutes, until dough is smooth and soft. Place dough in lightly oiled bowl, rolling ball over to cover with light film of oil. Cover bowl with cling film and place in warm spot to rise for 2 hours. Lightly oil 2 baking sheets, 25 x 38 cm (10 x 15 in). Divide dough into 4 equal pieces. Cover remaining pieces while you work with first portion. Using your hands, stretch dough into wide oval shape, about 30 x 15 cm (12 x 6 in) and 1 cm (½ in) thick. Place on baking sheet and cover with cling film. Repeat with remaining pieces. Using sharp knife, make 3 cuts on each side in chevron pattern, leaving a 5-cm (2-in) border at top and bottom and a 2.5-cm (1-in) border on sides. Using your finger, pull open the cuts, leaving a bit of space dividing the 4 strips. Cover in cling film and return to warm spot to rise for 30 minutes. Preheat oven to 200°C (400°F / Gas Mark 6). Lightly glaze loaves with olive oil and bake for 20 minutes, until golden brown and puffy. Repeat with remaining two loaves.

Makes 4. Serves 10–12.

focaccia

see variations page 161

Easy to make, this beautiful fluffy flatbread is perfect for sandwiches or enjoying with soup.

5 ml (1 tsp) sugar	225 g (8 oz) plain flour
7 g. (¼ oz) sachet active dried yeast	30 ml (2 tbsp) extra-virgin olive oil
75 ml (5 tbsp) warm water	5 ml (1 tsp) sea salt

Dissolve sugar and yeast in warm water. Set aside for 10 minutes. In large bowl of standing mixer, combine yeast mixture with flour. Mix until all flour is incorporated. Change to dough hook attachment and knead for 1 to 2 minutes until dough is smooth.

Place dough in lightly oiled bowl, turning ball over to lightly coat with oil. Cover with a damp cloth and set aside in a warm spot for 30 to 40 minutes, until dough has doubled in volume.

Preheat oven to 240°C (475°F / Gas Mark 9). Place dough on lightly floured board and knock back once. Knead briefly, then shape the dough into a long flat rectangle with rounded corners, about 23 x 28 cm (9 x 11 in). Brush olive oil over surface and sprinkle with sea salt.

Place on a baking sheet lined with baking paper or use pizza peel to transfer to preheated baking stone in bottom of oven. Bake for 10 to 15 minutes until lightly golden.

Makes 1. Serves 2–4.

ciabatta

see variations page 162

This Italian "slipper bread" is made with a starter dough, called "biga". Prepare the starter dough the day before you plan to bake your ciabatta.

biga
0.5 ml (⅛ tsp) active dried yeast
30 ml (2 tbsp) warm water
75 ml (5 tbsp) tepid water
125 g (4½ oz) strong white bread flour

ciabatta
2.5 ml (½ tsp) active dried yeast
30 ml (2 tbsp) warm milk
150 ml (5 fl oz) tepid water
15 ml (1 tbsp) olive oil
125 g (4½ oz) bread flour
115 g (4 oz) plain flour
7.5 (1½ tsp) salt

To prepare the biga, combine yeast and warm water in small bowl and set aside for 5 minutes. In a medium bowl, stir yeast mixture with tepid water and flour for 3 to 4 minutes, until smooth. Cover bowl with cling film and leave to stand at room temperature for 12 to 24 hours. To prepare the ciabatta, combine yeast and warm milk in small bowl. Stir and set aside for 5 minutes. In large bowl of standing mixer, combine biga, yeast mixture, tepid water, oil, and flour. Mix until dough begins to come together. Add salt, change to dough hook attachment, and knead dough for 4 minutes. Ciabatta dough is supposed to be sticky. Do not add more flour! Transfer dough to a lightly oiled bowl and cover with cling film. Place in a warm spot to rise for 2 hours, or until dough has doubled in volume. Turn risen dough onto a lightly floured board or counter. Using a sharp knife, cut dough in half. Shape each

piece into a large oblong slipper shape, roughly 23–25 cm (9–10 in) long. Cover with damp paper towel and return to warm spot to rise for additional 2 hours, until dough has doubled again. Place baking stone or quarry tiles on bottom rack in electric oven or on bottom of gas oven. Preheat to 220°C (425°F / Gas Mark 7) for 1 hour before baking. Lightly dust pizza peel with flour and set first loaf on peel. Gently shake ciabatta from the peel onto the stone or tiles. Repeat quickly with second loaf. Bake for 20 minutes, until loaves are a light golden colour. Slide pizza peel under loaves one at a time to remove from oven and transfer to wire rack to cool.

Makes 2. Serves 4–6.

hono

see variations page 163

This Swedish bread takes on many incarnations, but almost all involve the use of rye flour and anise seed.

15 ml (1 tbsp) active dried yeast
350 ml (1½ fl. oz.) warm water
15 ml (1 tbsp) aniseed
15 ml (1 tbsp) fennel seeds
30 ml (2 tbsp) grated orange zest
75 g (3 oz) molasses

65 g (2½ oz) sugar
15 ml (1 tbsp) salt
275 g (10 oz) rye flour
25 g (1 oz) unsalted butter, softened
275-350 g (10-12 oz) cups plain flour
fine cornmeal, for dusting

Sprinkle yeast over warm water in large bowl of standing mixer and set aside for 10 minutes. Add aniseed and fennel seeds, orange zest, molasses, sugar and salt; stir to blend. Add rye flour and butter; mix until all flour is incorporated. Add plain flour and change to dough hook attachment. Knead for 4 to 5 minutes, and transfer dough to lightly oiled bowl, rolling to cover dough with thin film of oil. Cover bowl with cling film and place in warm spot to rise for 2 hours, until dough has doubled in volume. Knead by hand for 2 minutes. Cut dough in half. Lightly oil 2 large rectangular baking sheets and dust with cornmeal. Using your hands, stretch dough into a wide oval shape. Place on baking sheet and cover with a clean damp kitchen towel. Repeat with second piece. Return to warm spot to rise for an additional hour. Preheat oven to 190°C (375°F / Gas Mark 5). Using a sharp knife, make 3 to 4 diagonal slits in the top of each loaf. Bake for 30 to 35 minutes, until loaves are brown on top. Tap bottom crust; if it sounds hollow, the bread is done. Transfer to a wire rack to cool.

Makes 2. Serves 8–10.

lefse

see variations page 164

Variations of this Norwegian potato flatbread abound – many families have their own favourite recipes. It is commonly served at most Norwegian holidays.

900 g (2 lb) potatoes, peeled, cooked, and finely
    mashed or riced
50 g (2 oz) unsalted butter, cut into
    small squares

120 ml (4 fl oz) whipping cream
10 ml (2 tsp) sugar
5 ml (1 tsp) salt
175 g (6 oz) plain flour

While your potatoes are still warm, add the butter and stir until it has completely melted and is well blended. Set aside to cool to room temperature. Add remaining ingredients, stirring until all the flour is incorporated and you have a smooth dough. Knead for 1 to 2 minutes. Shape into 16 to 18 patties, then flatten each into a round, 2-cm-thick (1-in). Place them on a baking sheet. Set aside for 5 minutes. Preheat an electric frying pan or lefse grill to the maximum setting. Lightly flour your rolling surface and rolling pin. Roll each patty out to a 30-cm (12-in) round, it doesn't have to be a perfect circle. Traditional lefse rolling pins are corrugated; their grooves prevent sticking. If your dough sticks to the rolling pin, place a large sheet of cling film over your patty and then roll over it. Peel off the cling film, slide a long metal spatula under the lefse to make sure it is not sticking to the work service, then carefully transfer it to the hot pan or grill, lifting it from the middle. Cook the lefse, in batches, for 30 seconds per side, until golden brown spots begin to appear on the underside. Transfer cooked lefse to clean paper towel to cool. Stack them if you like, but interleaf each with a sheet of paper towel. Lefse can be folded and stored in freezer for up to 6 months.

Makes 16–18. Serves 4–6.

crisp rye flatbread

see variations page 165

This crisp flatbread, known as "knackebrod" in Norway, became popular because it dries well and can be stored for long periods of time.

15 ml (1 tbsp) active dried yeast
225 ml (8 fl oz) warm water
160 g (5¼ oz) rye flour

160 g (5¼ oz) plain flour
5 ml (1 tsp) salt
40g (1½ oz) pumpernickel flour

Sprinkle yeast over warm water in a small bowl and set aside for 5 minutes. Combine flours and salt in large bowl of standing mixer. Incorporate yeast mixture on slow speed until dough begins to form.

Change to dough hook attachment and knead on slow speed, for 3 to 4 minutes, adding pumpernickel flour as necessary to make a smooth dough. Lightly flour board or counter with pumpernickel flour.

Turn dough onto surface and roll into a log. Slice log into 12 equal pieces and shape each piece into a ball. Place balls on baking sheet, cover with a clean paper towel, and place in a warm spot to rise for 30 minutes.

Preheat oven to 220°C (425°F / Gas Mark 7). Lightly oil 2 large rectangular baking sheets. Using a rolling pin, roll out each ball to form a 10-cm (4-in) disc. Place discs on baking sheets, prick surface with a fork, and bake for 8 to 10 minutes, until lightly browned. Transfer to wire rack to cool.

Makes 12. Serves 4–6.

bliny

see variations page 166

Bliny are Russian pancakes, made with a yeasted dough. They are traditionally served with a minced meat or sour cream filling; however, they have become quite popular in the West when served with crème fraiche and smoked salmon or caviar.

115 g (4 oz) plain flour
5 ml (1 tsp) salt
175 ml (6 fl oz) milk
6.25 ml (1¼ tsp) active dried yeast

2 large eggs, separated
75 ml (5 tbsp) sour cream, crème fraiche, or
   whipping cream
rapeseed oil, for greasing pan

Combine flour and salt in a medium bowl. Warm the milk in a saucepan. Remove from heat and sprinkle yeast over. Add egg yolks and sour cream to saucepan. Stir to blend. Slowly pour milk mixture into flour, stirring until batter is smooth. Cover bowl with cling film and place in a warm spot to rise for 1½ hours, until batter is foamy.

Beat egg whites in standing mixer with whisk attachment, until soft peaks form. Carefully fold egg whites into batter. Cover with cling film and return to warm spot for additional 2 hours.

To cook bliny, lightly coat a large frying pan with rapeseed oil. Pour 45 ml (3 tbsp) batter for small bliny or 90 ml (6 tbsp) for large onto hot frying pan and cook for 30 seconds to 1 minute per side, depending on the size of your bliny, until golden brown. Serve hot with topping of your choice.

Makes 10–12 small or 6 large bliny. Serves 2–3.

norwegian cracker bread

see variations page 167

This delicious cracker bread makes an excellent accompaniment for soups and dips.

125 g (4½ oz) wholemeal flour
175-350 g (6-12 oz) plain flour
5 ml (1 tsp) bicarbonate of soda
1.25 ml (¼ tsp) salt

225 ml (8 fl oz) buttermilk
120 ml (4 fl oz) whipping cream
175 g (6 oz) golden syrup

In a large bowl, mix the wholemeal flour with 175 g (6 oz) of the plain flour. Add the bicarbonate of soda, and salt. Stir in remaining ingredients until well incorporated into a smooth dough. Add up to 175 g (6 oz) of additional flour, 25 g (1 oz) at a time, until dough stiffens.

Divide dough into 6 equal pieces. Place first ball on lightly floured board. Cover remaining pieces with moistened paper towel to prevent drying. Using rolling pin, roll dough to form a paper-thin rectangle with rounded corners, measuring roughly 28 x 20 cm (11 x 8 in).

Preheat large electric frying pan to 180°C (350°F / Gas Mark 5). Transfer rolled dough to skillet and cook for 1 minute on each side. Repeat with 5 other pieces of dough. Preheat oven to 125°C (250°F / Gas Mark 3).

Place cracker breads in a single layer on baking sheets and bake for 10 minutes, or until crisp. To serve, break each piece into 4 crackers.

Makes 24. Serves 10–12.

oatcakes

see variations page 168

These Scottish oatcakes are served in wedges, known as "farls".

75 g (4¹/₂ oz) fine oatmeal (not rolled oats)
1.25 ml (¹/₄ tsp) salt
5 ml (1 tsp) salted butter, melted
75 ml (5 tbsp) boiling water

Set two large cast-iron frying pans to warm over medium heat on the hob.

Blend oatmeal and salt in medium bowl. Stir melted butter into the boiling water and pour into oatmeal mixture, until all dry ingredients are moistened. Add more boiling water if necessary, 15 ml (1 tbsp) at a time.

Lightly dust a wooden board or counter with oatmeal. Working quickly to prevent the dough from drying out, form 2 equal balls with the dough. Roll each one to a 15–20-cm (6–8-in) disc.

Using a sharp knife, cut into quarters and place the wedges in pre-heated pans.

Cook over medium heat for 3 to 5 minutes, until wedges begin to brown. Flip wedges over and cook for 1 minute more. Serve warm.

Makes 8. Serves 2–4.

barley breakfast bread

see variations page 169

This breakfast bread is easy to make – just make sure to soak the barley overnight for the most tender and flavourful results.

400 g (14 oz) pearl barley
500 ml (18 fl oz) buttermilk
225 ml (8 fl oz) water

300 g (10½ oz) barley flour
5 ml (1 tsp) baking soda
5 ml (1 tsp) salt

Rinse barley and place in large bowl with buttermilk. Cover with cling film and place in refrigerator to soak overnight.

In the morning, preheat oven to 180°C (350°F / Gas Mark 4). Grease and flour an 20-cm (8-in) cast-iron frying pan with an ovenproof handle.

Stir water into barley mixture and, using handheld immersion blender or standing blender, reduce barley to fine particles.

Add remaining ingredients and pour the batter into the pan. Tilt to level the surface. Place the pan in the oven and bake for 45 to 50 minutes. Turn onto a wire rack and leave to cool.

Makes one 20-cm (8-in) loaf. Serves 6–8.

variations

classic fougasse

see base recipe page 143

fougasse with sun-dried tomatoes
Prepare the basic recipe, replacing the olives with an equal quantity
of drained and chopped sun-dried tomatoes.

fougasse with walnuts
Prepare the basic recipe, replacing the olive oil with an equal quantity
of toasted walnut oil and replacing the olives with 115 g (4 oz) coarsely
chopped walnuts.

wholemeal fougasse
Prepare the basic recipe, replacing the buckwheat flour with an
equal quantity of wholemeal pastry flour.

fougasse with chili peppers
Prepare the basic recipe, adding 2 seeded and chopped large jalapeño
chillies with the olives.

fougasse with rosemary
Prepare the basic recipe, adding 5 ml (1 tsp) dried and crumbled rosemary
with the olives. Crumbled rosemary can also be added to taste after glazing
the dough with olive oil.

variations

focaccia

see base recipe page 144

focaccia with summer vegetables
Prepare the basic recipe, spreading summer vegetable topping over dough
prior to baking. To prepare topping, combine 30 ml (2 tbsp) extra-virgin olive
oil with 30 ml (2 tbsp) balsamic vinegar. Brush mixture over 175 g (6 oz)
courgette and I red onion cut in 1-cm (¼-in) slices, and 1 quartered yellow
pepper. Grill courgette for 4 minutes per side; peppers and onions 6 minutes
per side. Cool and slice peppers. Arrange vegetables over dough and top with
45 ml (3 tbsp) grated pecorino romano cheese.

focaccia with caramelized onions
Prepare the basic recipe, spreading caramelized onions over the dough prior to
baking. To prepare the onions, cook 4 thinly sliced mild onions in 75 ml (5 tbsp)
extra virgin olive oil in large frying pan over low heat until soft and caramelized.
Add 30 ml (2 tbsp) balsamic vinegar and season with salt and pepper.

cheese focaccia
Prepare the basic recipe, omitting the sea salt and adding 45 ml (3 tbsp)
grated pecorino romano cheese over the olive oil prior to baking.

focaccia with sage
Prepare the basic recipe, sprinkling 15 ml (1 tbsp) fresh chopped sage over
the focaccia with the sea salt.

variations

ciabatta

see base recipe page 146

cheese ciabatta
Prepare the basic recipe, adding 50 g (2 oz) grated cheddar cheese to the
dough before kneading.

ciabatta with sea salt
Prepare the basic recipe, dusting the tops of the loaves with 15 ml (1 tbsp)
coarse sea salt before baking.

ciabatta with flax seeds
Prepare the basic recipe, adding 35 g (1¼ oz) flax seeds to the dough
before kneading.

thyme ciabatta
Prepare the basic recipe, adding 1.25 ml (¼ tsp) dried and crumbled thyme
to the dough before kneading.

ciabatta with smoked paprika
Prepare the basic recipe, adding 1.25 ml (¼ tsp) smoked paprika to the
dough before kneading.

hono

see base recipe page 148

hono with celery seeds
Prepare the basic recipe, replacing the fennel seeds with an equal quantity of celery seeds.

hono with sunflower seeds
Prepare the basic recipe, replacing the fennel seeds with the same quantity of sunflower seeds.

hono with barley
Prepare the basic recipe, replacing 50 g (2 oz) plain flour with the same quantity of barley flour.

hono with cheese
Prepare the basic recipe, adding 45 ml (3 tbsp) finely grated Parmesan to the dough before kneading it.

hono with caraway seeds
Prepare the basic recipe, replacing the fennel seeds with an equal quantity of caraway seeds.

variations

lefse

see base recipe page 149

lefse with chives
Prepare the basic recipe, adding 30 ml (2 tbsp) finely chopped fresh chives
to the potato mixture before kneading.

cheese lefse
Prepare the basic recipe, adding 50 g (2 oz) grated cheddar cheese to the
potato mixture before kneading.

lefse with corn
Prepare the basic recipe, adding 115 g (4 oz) canned cream-style corn to the
potato mixture before kneading.

lefse with garlic
Prepare the basic recipe, adding 1 to 2 crushed garlic cloves to the
potato mixture before kneading.

crisp rye flatbread

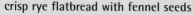

see base recipe page 151

crisp rye flatbread with fennel seeds
Prepare the basic recipe, adding 10 ml (2 tsp) fennel seeds with the flour.

crisp rye flatbread with flax seeds
Prepare the basic recipe, adding 10 ml (2 tsp) flax seeds with the flour.

crisp rye flatbread with cheese
Prepare the basic recipe, sprinkling 5-10 ml (1-2 tsp) finely grated Parmesan over each disc before baking them.

crisp rye flatbread with sesame seeds
Prepare the basic recipe, sprinkling 1.25 ml (¼ tsp) sesame seeds over each disc before baking them.

crisp rye flatbread with herring
Prepare the basic recipe, garnishing each flatbread with a few pieces of pickled herring and a pinch of chopped fresh dill.

variations

bliny

see base recipe page 152

wholemeal bliny
Prepare the basic recipe, replacing 50 g (2 oz) plain flour with
wholemeal flour.

bliny with grated apple
Prepare the basic recipe, adding 50 g (2 oz) grated apple
to the batter before cooking.

bliny with grated potato
Prepare the basic recipe, adding 50 g (2 oz) and grated potato
to the batter before cooking.

bliny with raisins
Prepare the basic recipe, adding 40 g (1½ oz) small golden raisins
to the batter before cooking.

buckwheat bliny
Prepare the basic recipe, replacing 50 g (2 oz) plain flour
with buckwheat flour.

variations

norwegian cracker bread

see base recipe page 155

norwegian cracker bread with fleur de sel
Prepare the basic recipe, sprinkling each piece with 15 ml (1 tbsp)
fleur de sel before baking in oven.

norwegian cracker bread with flax seeds
Prepare the basic recipe, adding 10 ml (2 tsp) flax seeds to the
flour mixture.

norwegian cracker bread with parmesan
Prepare the basic recipe, sprinkling each piece with 15 ml (1 tbsp) finely
grated Parmesan before baking in oven.

norwegian cracker bread with gorgonzola
Prepare the basic recipe, serving each cracker with a wedge of Gorgonzola
topped with a slice of green apple.

norwegian cracker bread with oregano
Prepare the basic recipe, adding 5 ml (1 tsp) dried oregano to the
flour mixture.

oatcakes

see base recipe page 156

oatcakes with strawberry jam
Prepare the basic recipe, spreading 15 ml (1 tbsp) strawberry jam over each farl before serving.

oatcakes with aged cheddar
Prepare the basic recipe, topping each farl with a 25 g (1 oz) wedge of aged cheddar before serving.

oatcakes with marmite
Prepare the basic recipe, spreading each farl with 2.5 ml (½ tsp) marmite before serving.

oatcakes with onion chutney
Prepare the basic recipe, topping each farl with 5 ml (1 tsp) onion chutney before serving.

oatcakes with bran
Prepare the basic recipe, adding 25 g (1 oz) bran flakes to the oatmeal mixture. Add more water to recipe if necessary.

variations

barley breakfast bread

see base recipe page 159

barley bread with butter & jam
Prepare the basic recipe, spreading 5 ml (1 tsp) butter and 5 ml (1 tsp) raspberry jam over each slice before serving.

barley & spelt bread
Prepare the basic recipe, replacing 65 g (2½ oz) barley flour with spelt flour.

barley & quinoa bread
Prepare the basic recipe, replacing 65 g (2½ oz) barley flour with quinoa flour.

barley & oat bread
Prepare the basic recipe, replacing 65 g (2½ oz) barley flour with the same quantity of fine oatmeal.

barley breakfast bread with dried apricots
Prepare the basic recipe, adding 115 g (4 oz) chopped dried apricots to the dough with the remaining ingredients before baking.

indian &
african
flatbreads

This chapter contains every kind of texture

you could hope to find in flatbreads – from soft

naan to crispy poppadum and chewy coconut

rotis. Experiment to see which ones pair the

best with your favorite spicy dishes.

naan

see variations page 188

This addictive flatbread is the perfect complement to any curry dish. Naan is traditionally baked by being slapped onto the wall of a tandoor oven.

7.5 ml (1–2 tsp) active dry yeast
225 ml (8 fl oz) warm water
50 g (2 oz) sugar
45 ml (3 tbsp) whole milk
1 large egg, lightly beaten

10 ml (2 tsp) salt
500 g (1 lb 2 oz) strong white bread flour
1 garlic clove, peeled
50 g (2 oz) unsalted butter

In large bowl of standing mixer, sprinkle yeast over warm water. Set aside for 10 minutes, until yeast becomes foamy. Add sugar, milk, egg, salt, and flour; mix well. Change to dough hook attachment and knead for 4 to 5 minutes, until dough is smooth. Place in lightly oiled bowl, rolling dough over to cover with thin film of oil. Cover bowl with a clean damp paper towel and place in a warm spot to rise for 1 hour, or until dough has doubled in volume. Knock dough back once to deflate. Using sharp knife, cut into 14 egg-sized pieces. Roll into 14 balls and place on lightly oiled baking sheet. Cover with paper towel and return to warm spot for additional 30 minutes. Place baking stone or quarry tiles on bottom rack of oven and preheat to 230°C (450°F / Gas Mark 8). Lightly flour pizza peel. Using fingers or rolling pin, shape dough into oblong shapes, roughly 15 x 10 cm (6 x 4 in). Place first naan on pizza peel and gently shake it onto baking stone. Repeat with as many naan as will fit on tiles. Bake for 8 to 10 minutes, until puffy with golden brown spots. While naan are baking, melt butter over low heat with garlic. Brush hot naan with butter as they come out of oven. Repeat until all naan have been baked.

Makes 14. Serves 6–8.

chapatti

see variations page 189

This thin flatbread can be used to make wraps or to be served with curry or dhal.

125 g (4 1/2 oz) wholemeal
115 g (4 oz) plain flour
5 ml (1 tsp) salt
30 ml (2 tbsp) olive oil
175 ml (6 fl oz) hot water

Combine flours and salt in large bowl. Make a well in the centre and stir in olive oil and just enough water to make a soft dough. Turn dough onto a lightly floured surface and knead until it is smooth and elastic.

Use a sharp knife to cut the dough into 10 equal pieces. Shape each piece into a ball and place on a baking sheet. Set aside for 30 minutes.

Heat a large heavy frying pan or *tava*. Lightly coat with oil. On a lightly floured board or counter, roll dough out to a roughly 20-cm (8-in) round.

Place chapatti on hot pan and cook for 30 seconds per side, until brown spots appear. Repeat with remaining balls of dough. Wrap the cooked chapatti with clean paper towel to keep them soft as they cool. Serve warm or at room temperature.

Makes 10. Serves 4–5.

poppadum

see variations page 190

These crisp lentil-based flatbreads must be allowed to dry for several days before they are fried, toasted or broiled.

25 g (1 oz) mung dhal (lentils) finely ground
1.25 ml ($^1/_4$ tsp) freshly ground black pepper
1.25 ml ($^1/_4$ tsp) finely ground chilli powder
75 ml (5 tbsp) water

Place all ingredients in a saucepan and cook over medium heat for 3 minutes, until water has been completely absorbed. Cool to room temperature. Divide dough into 8 equal portions and shape into balls. Place a sheet of cling film or baking paper on a board. Place a dough ball on top and cover with another sheet. Roll the ball into a paper-thin 10-cm (4-in) round. Repeat with the other balls.

Place rounds on a wire rack to dry for 24 hours at room temperature or outside in hot summer sun. Turn poppadum over and continue to dry them for 3 more days. Store dried poppadums in an airtight container.

To serve poppadum, heat rapeseed oil to a depth of 5 cm (2 in) in a deep frying pan. Use tongs to place poppadum in hot oil. Cook for 10 seconds, remove, and place on wire rack to drain and cool. Alternatively, brush with oil and cook under a pre-heated grill for a few seconds.

Makes 8. Serves 2–3.

sri lankan coconut roti

see variations page 191

These sweet flatbreads make a pleasing addition to a spicy meal.

225 g (8 oz) plain flour
2.5 ml (½ tsp) salt
125 g (4½ oz) dessicated coconut
60 ml (4 tbsp) boiling water
15 g (½ oz) unsalted butter

Combine flour, salt, and coconut in large bowl. Add enough boiling water to make a soft dough that is not sticky. Turn dough onto lightly floured surface and knead for 5 minutes.

Divide the dough into 12 egg-sized pieces, then flatten each one into a 7.5-cm (3-in) disc. Place each disc in turn between 2 sheets of cling film or baking paper and roll out to form a circular roti, about 2 mm (¹/₁₂ in) thick.

Preheat the oven to 140°C (275°F / Gas Mark 1). Preheat a large heavy frying pan over high heat. When the frying pan is very hot, peel a roti off the paper and place it in the pan. Cook for 1 minute per side, until the roti begins to brown.

Remove and place on an ovenproof plate in the oven to keep warm until serving time. Cook the remaining roti in the same way.

Makes 12. Serves 4–6.

parathas

see variations page 192

These fried flatbreads are folded twice; the four layers result in a delightfully flaky texture.

250 g (8 oz) wholemeal pastry flour
176 g (6 oz) plain flour
5 ml (1 tsp) sea salt

45 ml (3 tbsp) rapeseed oil
225 ml (8 fl oz) warm water
115 g (4 oz) unsalted butter, melted

Combine the wholemeal flour and 115 g (4 oz) fo the plain flour with salt in the large bowl of standing mixer. Make a well in the centre of the flour mixture and pour in the rapeseed oil. Rub oil into the flour by picking up a portion of the flour and oil with your right hand, picking up some flour with your left hand, and sliding your left hand from palm to fingers over your right hand. Repeat until all the flour is moistened and no lumps of oil remain. Return the bowl to the mixer and add the warm water, stirring on slow speed until dough forms. Change to the dough hook and knead dough for 5 to 6 minutes, until it is very soft and smooth. Cover bowl with cling film and place in a warm spot for 30 minutes. Turn dough onto a lightly floured board or counter. Knead dough briefly by hand, 1 to 2 minutes, then divide in half. Using your hands, roll each piece into a log. With a sharp knife, cut each log into 8 equal pieces and shape each into a small ball. Dust balls with remaining plain flour, place in bowl and cover with a clean damp kitchen cloth to prevent drying. Place one ball of dough on lightly floured board. Flatten into a disc, dust both sides with flour, then roll out to a 13-cm (5-in) round. Brush the top with melted butter and fold in half. Again, glaze the top of the half-moon shape with melted butter and fold in half. Lightly dust both sides

of the triangular patty with flour and roll out until you have a 18-cm (7-in) triangle. Repeat process with the other 15 balls of dough. Preheat oven to 140°C (275°F / Gas Mark 1). Heat large cast-iron frying pan on a hot burner. When frying pan is hot, cook first triangle of dough for 2 minutes, until golden brown spots appear on bottom. Flip and cook for 15 to 20 seconds. Brush with melted butter, flip and cook for 30 seconds. Brush second side and repeat. Transfer parathas to ovenproof dish and place in oven to keep warm. Repeat with remaining triangles of dough.

Makes 16. Serves 6–8.

dosas

see variations page 193

Dosas, traditionally served as breakfast food, are made from a batter of split, skinned urad beans that have soaked overnight. It is important to use the creamy white split beans and not the strong flavoured and tougher black beans, and to soak the beans overnight.

175 g (6 oz) split and skinned urad beans
900 ml (1½ pints) water, plus more for soaking
275 g (10 oz) rice flour

5 ml (1 tsp) salt
15 ml (1 tbsp) rapeseed oil

Place beans in small bowl. Cover with water and leave to soak 10 to 12 hours at room temperature. Drain the beans and purée in a blender, adding up to 225 ml (8 fl oz) water as necessary to make a smooth paste. In small saucepan over low heat, warm 120 ml (4 fl oz) water. Add 15 ml (1 tbsp) rice flour and whisk until it thickens. Remove from heat and set aside. Combine bean purée, salt, remaining rice flour, and remaining measured water in large bowl of standing mixer. Mix on medium speed until batter is smooth and thin. Reduce speed to slow and incorporate reserved rice flour mixture. When batter is smooth, cover with cling film and set aside for 6 to 12 hours.

Preheat oven to 140°C (275°F / Gas Mark 1). Lightly oil and preheat a large heavy-bottomed frying pan. When pan is hot, pour 120 ml (4 fl oz) batter onto center of pan, tilting the pan in an up-and-down, side-to-side motion to help spread the batter to a thin 20–25-cm (8–10-in) round. Cook for 1 to 2 minutes per side, until dosa is golden brown and crispy around the edges. Place cooked dosa on an ovenproof plate and keep warm in oven while you cook the remaining dosas.

Make 16–18. Serves 5–6.

injera

see variations page 194

This spongy Ethiopian flatbread is made from a batter that has fermented for at least 24 hours. Injera is the ultimate finger food; it is placed on the plate beneath several portions of various stews and is used to scoop up mouthfuls.

5 ml (1 tsp) active dried yeast
750 ml (1¼ pints) warm water
225 g (8 oz) teff flour

In small bowl, sprinkle yeast over 120 ml (4 fl oz) warm water. Set aside for 5 minutes. Place flour in large bowl of standing mixer. Add the remaining warm water and stir to combine. Stir in yeast mixture. Cover bowl with cling film and leave to ferment at room temperature for 24 to 72 hours.

Preheat a large heavy-based frying pan. When frying pan is hot, pour 120 ml (4 fl oz) batter onto centre of pan, tilting the pan in an up-and-down, side-to-side motion to help spread the batter to a thin 25–30-cm (10–12-in) round. Unlike pancakes, injera only cook on one side.

Cook for 2 minutes over low heat, until surface is spongy and cratered and edges are curling up slightly. Transfer to a plate to cool. Make more injera in the same way.

Makes 6–8. Serves 3–4.

chickpea flatbread

see variations page 195

This healthy flatbread is the perfect addition to a tapas spread.

10 ml (2 tsp) active dry yeast
225 ml (8 fl oz) warm water
15 ml (1 tbsp) honey
450 g (1 lb) strong white bread flour

15 ml (1 tbsp) salt
225 g (8 oz) chickpeas, drained and mashed
7.5 ml (1½ tsp) cumin seeds, slightly crushed
7.5 ml (1½ tsp) coriander seeds, slightly crushed

In small bowl, sprinkle yeast over 120 ml (4 fl oz) warm water. Stir in honey. Set aside for 5 minutes. In large bowl of standing mixer, mix 225 g (8 oz) flour and salt. Add yeast mixture and mix on slow speed until incorporated. Add remaining flour, mashed chickpeas and seeds. Stir to combine. Add up to 120 ml (4 fl oz) more warm water and up to 50 g (2 oz) more bread flour to make a smooth, moist dough. Change to dough hook attachment and knead for 4 to 5 minutes. Place dough in lightly oiled bowl, rolling dough over to cover with a thin film of oil. Cover bowl with cling film and place in a warm spot to rise for 1 hour, or until doubled in volume.

Place baking stone on bottom rack and preheat oven to 230°C (450°F / Gas Mark 8). Knock dough back once to deflate, then divide into 5 equal pieces. Lightly flour pizza peel. Using fingers or rolling pin, shape dough into oblong shapes, roughly 5 mm (¼ in) thick. Place first flatbread on pizza peel and gently shake it onto baking stone.

Bake 2 to 3 flatbreads at a time, for 4 to 5 minutes, until they are puffy and golden brown. Transfer to a wire rack to cool slightly.

Makes 5. Serves 6–8.

spicy moroccan flatbread with olives

see variations page 196

This flatbread, made without yeast, is covered with an exquisite blend of seasonings.

125 g (4¹/₂ oz) plain flour
10 ml (2 tsp) sugar
5 ml (1 tsp) salt
1.25 ml (¹/₄ tsp) freshly ground black
    pepper
10 Moroccan olives, drained, pitted, and
    coarsely chopped

15 ml (1 tbsp) extra-virgin olive oil, plus
    more for glazing
120 ml (4 fl oz) water
1.25 ml (¹/₄ tsp) salt
2.5 ml (¹/₂ tsp) garlic powder
1.25 ml (¹/₄ tsp) curry powder
1.25 ml (¹/₄ tsp) ground cumin

In large bowl of standing mixer, combine flour, sugar, salt, pepper and chopped olives. Stir in 1 tablespoon of olive oil. Add water and mix until dough forms a ball. Change to dough hook attachment and knead for 1 to 2 minutes, until dough is smooth. Cover bowl with cling film and refrigerate for 1 hour. To prepare spice blend, combine the remaining ingredients in a small bowl. Set aside. Preheat oven to 200°C (400°F / Gas Mark 6) and line a large rectangular baking sheet with baking paper. Lightly wipe paper with olive oil. Turn dough onto lightly floured board or counter. Using rolling pin, roll dough into a paper-thin oblong shape. Carefully transfer dough to baking sheet. Lightly glaze flatbread with olive oil and sprinkle with spice blend. Place baking sheet on rack in middle of oven and bake for 20 minutes, until flatbread is golden brown. Transfer to wire rack to cool. Break into pieces to serve.

Makes 1. Serves 4–5 as an appetizer.

cardamom flatbread

see variations page 197

Cardamom is the spice made from grinding the aromatic seeds from a plant in the ginger family. It lends a delicate flavour to this sweet stuffed flatbread.

dough
115 g (4 oz) plain flour
pinch of salt
22 ml (1½ tbsp) rapeseed oil, warmed
60 ml (4 tbsp) water

filling
25 g (1 oz) chickpea flour
5 ml (1 tsp) rapeseed oil
175 g (6 oz) brown sugar
15 ml (1 tbsp) poppy seeds
1.25 ml (¼ tsp) cardamom
pinch of nutmeg
25 ml (1 oz) unsalted butter, melted

To prepare dough, combine flour, salt, and 15 ml (1 tbsp) oil in large bowl of standing mixer. Add just enough water to form stiff dough. Change to dough hook attachment and knead for 2 minutes. Set aside for 10 minutes. Knead again, adding remaining oil to soften dough. Form dough into balls the size of small peach. To prepare filling, cook chickpea flour in rapeseed oil until golden. Combine chickpea flour mixture with brown sugar, poppy seeds, cardamom and nutmeg. Knead by hand and form walnut-sized balls. Flatten 2 dough balls into discs. Flatten a ball of filling and sandwich it between the discs. Using rolling pin, roll sandwich into thin disc, 13–15 cm (5–6 in) wide. Repeat with rest of dough and filling. Preheat oven to 140°C (275°F / Gas Mark 1). Heat a large cast-iron or nonstick frying pan over medium heat. Cook flatbread for 2 minutes, or until bottom layer browns. Brush top layer with melted butter and cook for 1 minute more. Repeat until both sides are golden brown. Repeat until all dough is used up. Serve warm.

Makes 3–4. Serves 3–4.

variations

naan

see base recipe page 171

naan with cumin
Prepare the basic recipe, adding 5 ml (1 tsp) ground cumin with the flour. Sprinkle a pinch of cumin seeds over each naan before baking.

naan with nigella seeds
Prepare the basic recipe, sprinkling each naan with a pinch of nigella seeds before baking.

garlic naan
Prepare the basic recipe, adding 1 crushed garlic clove with the flour.

naan with ghee
Prepare the basic recipe, replacing the unsalted butter with an equal quantity of ghee.

variations

chapatti

see base recipe page 172

chapatti with ghee
Prepare the basic recipe, brushing each chapatti with ghee before serving.

millet chapatti
Prepare the basic recipe, replacing 55 g (2¼ oz) wholemeal flour with an equal quantity of millet flour.

corn flour chapatti
Prepare the basic recipe, replacing 55 g (2¼ oz) wholemeal flour with and equal quanity of fine cornmeal.

wholemeal chapatti
Prepare the basic recipe, replacing the plain flour with 125 g (4½ oz) wholemeal flour.

variations

poppadum

see base recipe page 175

poppadum with pink peppercorns
Prepare the basic recipe, adding 1.25 ml (¼ tsp) crushed pink peppercorns.

poppadum with cayenne
Prepare the basic recipe, adding a pinch of cayenne pepper.

poppadum with cumin
Prepare the basic recipe, adding 1.25 ml (¼ tsp) ground cumin.

poppadum with garlic
Prepare the basic recipe, adding 1.25 ml (¼ tsp) garlic powder.

variations

sri lankan coconut roti

see base recipe page 176

sri lankan coconut roti with raspberry jam

Prepare the basic recipe, spreading each roti with 5-10 ml (1-2 tsp) raspberry jam before serving.

sri lankan coconut roti with honey

Prepare the basic recipe, spreading each roti with 15 ml (1 tbsp) honey before serving.

sri lankan coconut roti with treacle

Prepare the basic recipe, spreading each roti with 15 ml (1 tbsp) treacle before serving.

sri lankan coconut with banana

Prepare the basic recipe, topping each roti with several slices of fresh banana.

variations

parathas

see base recipe page 178

parathas with potatoes

Prepare the basic recipe, topping each paratha with 15-30 ml (1-2 tbsp)
prepared potato curry.

parathas with egg

Prepare the basic recipe, topping each paratha with 15-30 ml (1-2 tbsp)
scrambled egg.

parathas with chutney

Prepare the basic recipe, topping each paratha with 15-30 ml (1-2 tbsp)
chutney.

parathas with pomegranate seeds

Prepare the basic recipe, topping each paratha with 15 ml (1 tbsp)
pomegranate seeds.

variations

dosas

see base recipe page 180

semolina dosas

Prepare the basic recipe, replacing 65 g (2½ oz) rice flour with fine semolina flour.

dosas with omelette

Prepare the basic recipe, placing 50 g (2 oz) omelette in the middle of each dosa. Fold the top and bottom over the filling and roll the dosa up, as you would a burrito.

dosas with ghee

Prepare the basic recipe, brushing each dosa with 15 ml (1 tbsp) ghee.

dosas with onions

Prepare the basic recipe, placing 45 ml (3 tbsp) caramelized onions in the middle of each dosa. Fold the top and bottom over the filling and roll the dosa up, as you would a burrito.

variations

injera

see base recipe page 181

wheat injera

Prepare the basic recipe, replacing teff flour with an equal quantity of
plain flour. Increase yeast to 10 ml (2 tsp). Reduce standing time
to 2 to 3 hours.

corn injera

Prepare the basic recipe, replacing 60 g (2 oz) teff flour with an equal
quantity of fine cornmeal.

barley injera

Prepare the basic recipe, replacing 60 g (2 oz) teff flour with an equal
quantity of barley flour.

rice injera

Prepare the basic recipe, replacing 60 g (2 oz) teff flour with an equal
quantity of rice flour.

variations

chickpea flatbread

see base recipe page 183

chickpea flatbread with saffron
Prepare the basic recipe, adding 2 ml (⅓ tsp) saffron threads steeped
in 60 ml (4 tbsp) warm water for 10 minutes with the mashed chickpeas.
Omit cumin and coriander seeds.

chickpea flatbread with smoked paprika
Prepare the basic recipe, adding 2.5 ml (½ tsp) smoked paprika with
the other spices.

chickpea flatbread with mint
Prepare the basic recipe, adding 2.5 ml (½ tsp) dried mint with the
other spices.

chickpea flatbread with ground pomegranate seeds
Prepare the basic recipe, adding 2.5 ml (½ tsp) ground pomegranate seeds
with the other seeds.

variations

spicy moroccan flatbread with olives

see base recipe page 184

spicy moroccan flatbread with sun-dried tomatoes
Prepare the basic recipe, replacing the olives with 40 g (1½ oz) drained and chopped sun-dried tomatoes.

spicy moroccan flatbread with figs
Prepare the basic recipe, replacing the olives with 40 g (1½ oz) chopped dried figs.

spicy moroccan flatbread with currants
Prepare the basic recipe, replacing the olives with 40 g (1½ oz) dried currants.

spicy moroccan flatbread with peppers
Prepare the basic recipe, replacing the olives with 40 g (1½ oz) chopped roasted red peppers.

cardamom flatbread

see base recipe page 187

cardamom & cinnamon flatbread
Prepare the basic recipe, adding 1.25 ml (¼ tsp) ground cinnamon
with the other spices.

cardamom & allspice flatbread
Prepare the basic recipe, adding a pinch of ground allspice with
the other spices.

cardamom chocolate flatbread
Prepare the basic recipe, adding 30 ml (2 tbsp) unsweetened cocoa
powder with the spices.

cardamom walnut flatbread
Prepare the basic recipe, adding 25 g (1 oz) finely chopped walnuts
to the filling.

flatbreads & hearth breads of the middle east

The flatbreads in this chapter are as diverse as the

countries they originate from. Whether you want

something soft and pliable or crisp and covered

in seeds, you are sure to find the perfect flatbread

to serve with your next Middle Eastern feast.

matzoh

see variations page 214

For matzoh to be considered kosher for Passover, it must finish baking within 18 minutes of the water having come into contact with the grain. This ensures that no fermentation has occurred.

250 g (9 oz) matzoh meal
2.5 ml (½ tsp) kosher salt
350 ml (12 fl oz) kosher spring water

Preheat oven to 230°C (450°F / Gas Mark 8) . In a large bowl, combine matzoh meal and salt. Pour in water and stir until a dough forms. Working quickly, turn dough onto a surface lightly floured with matzoh meal and knead for 3 to 4 minutes. Cut the dough into 8 equal pieces.

Working with one piece at a time, roll dough as thin as possible between 2 sheets of baking paper. Peel off top layer of baking paper and transfer other piece to large rectangular baking sheet. Cut dough into four 7.5-cm (3-in) squares. Prick surface of dough with fork or pastry docker.

Place in preheated oven and bake for 3 to 4 minutes, until golden and crisp. Transfer to wire rack to cool and dry. Repeat with remaining dough.

To meet time constraints, ensure that at least two people are preparing the matzohs.

Makes 32 matzoh squares

manakish

see variations page 215

This Lebanese specialty has become popular around the world. Topped with a delectable blend of thyme and sesame seeds, zahtar flatbread works well with other mezze dishes.

1 x 7 g (¼ oz) sachet active dried yeast
175 g (6 oz) plain flour
120 ml (4 fl oz) cup warm water
2.5 ml (1/2 tsp) salt

50 g (2 oz) dried thyme
50 g (2 oz) ground sumac
15 ml (1 tbsp) sesame seeds
45 ml (3 tbsp) extra-virgin olive oil

In a medium bowl, combine the yeast with 15 ml (1 tbsp) flour and 60 ml (4 tbsp) warm water. Stir and set aside for 10 minutes, until mixture becomes foamy. In large bowl of standing mixer, combine salt and 75 g (3 oz) flour. Add yeast mixture and remaining water. Mix until well incorporated. Add remaining flour and mix until dough begins to pull away from sides of bowl. Change to dough hook attachment and knead for 4 to 5 minutes, until dough is smooth and elastic. Shape dough into a ball, dust with flour, place in bowl, and cover with cling film. Place bowl in warm spot to rise for 1½ hours, until dough has doubled in volume. To prepare zahtar spice blend, combine the thyme, sumac, and sesame seeds in medium bowl. Stir in olive oil to form a paste. Place baking stone on lowest rack in oven and preheat to 180°C (350°F / Gas Mark 4). Turn dough onto lightly floured surface and roll out to form an oblong shape, roughly 30 x 20 cm (12 x 8 in). Spread a generous layer of the zahtar spice blend over flatbread. Lightly flour pizza peel. Place flatbread on pizza peel and gently shake it onto baking stone. Bake for 3 to 4 minutes, or until flatbread is golden brown and crispy around the edges. Serve warm.

Makes 1. Serves 2–3.

sangak

see variations page 216

In Iran, sangak is baked in a large oven over hot stones, giving it a unique texture.
This version is divided in smaller pieces to fit into domestic ovens.

15 ml (1 tbsp) active dried yeast
600 ml (1 pint) warm water
7.5 ml (1½ tsp) salt

385 g (13½ oz) wholemeal flour
115 g (4 oz) plain flour
60 ml (4 tbsp) sesame seeds

In a large bowl of standing mixer, sprinkle the yeast over 120 ml (4 fl oz) warm water. Set aside for 5 minutes. Stir in salt and 350 ml (12 fl oz) warm water, and set aside for 10 more minutes. Add flour, about 115 g (4 oz) at a time, and remaining water. Mix on low speed until dough is smooth. Place dough in lightly oiled bowl, cover with a damp paper towel, and place in a warm spot to rise for 3 hours, until dough has doubled in volume. Place baking stone on bottom rack and preheat oven to the highest temperature, usually 240°C (475°F / Gas Mark 9). Return dough to large bowl of standing mixer, and change to the dough hook attachment. Knead for 5 to 6 minutes. Using a sharp knife, divide the dough into 6 equal pieces. With fingers or rolling pin, stretch out dough to an oblong shape, 1 cm (1/2 in) thick. Lightly flour pizza peel. Place first flatbread on pizza peel. Dimple the surface with damp fingertips, sprinkle with 5 ml (1 tsp) sesame seeds, and gently shake it onto baking stone. Bake for 3 to 4 minutes, pressing the loaf down with the pizza peel to flatten it after the first minute. Slide pizza peel under the flatbread to remove from oven. Using tongs, flip the flatbread over and return to baking stone to bake for 2 minutes longer. Transfer to a wire rack to cool. Repeat with remaining flatbreads.

Makes 6. Serves 10–12.

barbari

see variations page 217

This long flatbread is known for its distinctive ridges.

60 ml (4 tbsp) warm water
10 ml (2 tsp) active dried yeast
550 g (1¼ lb) plain flour
7.5 ml (1½ tsp) salt
45 ml (3 tbsp) sugar

40 g (1½ oz) unsalted butter, melted
500 ml (18 fl oz) warm water
30 ml (2 tbsp) milk
60 ml (4 tbsp) sesame seeds

In small bowl, sprinkle yeast over 60 ml (4 tbsp) warm water. Stir and set aside for 5 minutes, until dissolved. Place flour in large bowl of standing mixer. Make well in center of flour and pour in yeast mixture, salt, sugar, melted butter, and water. Blend on slow speed. When flour is completely incorporated, change to dough hook attachment. Knead for 4 to 5 minutes, until dough is smooth and elastic. Shape dough into ball and place in lightly oiled bowl, rolling dough over to cover with thin film of oil. Cover with clean, damp paper towel and place in warm spot to rise for 1 hour, until doubled in volume. Place baking stone on lower rack and preheat oven to 180°C (350°F / Gas Mark 4) . Knock dough back once to deflate. Using sharp knife, cut dough into 4 equal pieces. Shape each piece into ball. Place on lightly floured board, dust with flour, cover, and return to warm spot for additional 20 minutes. Using fingers or rolling pin, stretch out each piece to form oblong shape, roughly 30 x 15 cm (12 x 6 in). Using the side of one thumb, make ridges from one end of loaf to other, leaving a 2-cm (1-in) border on all sides and spacing the ridges 2.5 cm (1 in) apart. Brush loaf with a quarter of the milk and sprinkle

with 15 ml (1 tbsp) of the sesame seeds. Prepare remaining three flatbreads and set aside for 15 minutes. Lightly flour pizza peel. Gently shake one flatbread from peel onto baking stone. Bake 2 at a time if space allows. Bake for 20 to 25 minutes, or until flatbread is puffy and golden brown. Transfer to wire rack to cool.

Makes 4. Serves 8–10.

pitta

see variations page 218

This popular flatbread, also known as pocket bread, is used to make stuffed sandwiches. If any of your pitta breads do not puff up sufficiently, use them for making pitta chips.

5 ml (1 tsp) active dried yeast
60 ml (4 tbsp) warm water
7.5 ml (½ tbsp) extra-virgin olive oil
7.5 ml (½ tbsp) honey

175 ml (6 fl oz) tepid water
115 g (4 oz) wholemeal flour
175 g (6 oz) plain flour
5 ml (1 tsp) salt

In small bowl, sprinkle yeast over 60 ml (4 tbsp) warm water. Stir and set aside for 5 minutes, until yeast has dissolved. Combine oil, honey, and tepid water in large bowl. Combine flours and salt in large measuring cup. With mixer on slow, incorporate flour mixture and yeast mixture into oil and honey mixture. Cover bowl with clean paper towel and set aside for 20 minutes. Sprinkle salt over dough, change to dough hook attachment, and knead for 4 to 5 minutes, until dough is smooth and elastic. Turn dough into clean bowl, cover, and place in warm spot to rise for 1½ to 2 hours, until dough has doubled in volume. Turn dough onto lightly floured surface. Using sharp knife, cut into 8 equal pieces. Shape each piece into ball, dust with flour, cover with clean damp paper towel, and set aside for 30 minutes. Place baking stone on lowest rack and preheat oven to 240°C (475°F / Gas Mark 9). Using rolling pin, roll out each ball to 15-cm (6-in) disc, 5 mm (¼ in) thick. Carefully place sheet of foil over the baking stone to diffuse heat slightly. Lightly flour pizza peel and gently shake pitta breads from peel onto foil-covered stone. Bake for 5 minutes, until pittas are golden and puffed up. Place large rectangle of foil on wire rack. Transfer baked pittas to foil and carefully wrap them up while they cool.

Makes 8. Serves 3–4.

lavash

see variations page 219

Lavash is a paper-thin Armenian flatbread that is soft and supple when warm and dry and brittle when cooled.

15 ml (1 tbsp) clear honey	385 g (13½ oz) strong unbleached
350 ml (12 fl oz) warm water	bread flour
2.5 ml (½ tsp) active dried yeast	5 ml (1 tsp salt)

In a small bowl, combine honey and warm water. Sprinkle yeast over water, stir, and set aside for 5 minutes, until dissolved. Place 225 g (8 oz) flour in large bowl of standing mixer. Make a well in the middle of the flour and pour in the yeast mixture. Mix on slow speed for 1 minute. Add salt and remaining flour. If dough is still soft, add up to 50 g (2 oz) more flour until you have a stiff dough. Change to dough hook attachment. Knead for 4 to 5 minutes, until dough is smooth and elastic. Turn dough into a clean bowl, cover with cling film, and place in a warm spot to rise for 3 hours, until dough has doubled in volume.

Knock down dough to deflate, then set aside for 10 minutes. Place baking stone or tiles on lowest rack and preheat oven to 230°C (450°F / Gas Mark 7). Turn dough onto lightly floured board or counter, and pat into a large rectangle. Using a sharp knife, cut dough into 8 equal square-shaped pieces. Keeping remaining pieces covered, roll first square out to a paper-thin rectangle, roughly 30 x 25 cm (12 x 10 in). Prick holes in dough with fork. Lightly flour pizza peel and gently transfer first piece of lavash to baking stone. Bake for 2 to 3 minutes, until pale brown. Transfer to wire rack to cool. Repeat with remaining pieces.

Makes 8. Serves 8–10.

garlic hearth bread

see variations page 220

This easy and aromatic hearth bread will satisfy the deepest craving for roasted garlic.

1 head fresh garlic, top removed
105 ml (7 tbsp) plus 5 ml (1 tsp) extra-virgin
   olive oil
400 g (14 oz) strong white bread flour

10 ml (2 tsp) easy-blend dried yeast
10 ml (2 tsp) salt
325 ml (11 fl oz) warm water

To prepare roasted garlic, preheat oven to 190°C (375°F / Gas Mark 5). Place head of garlic on large square of foil. Drizzle oil over garlic and wrap foil around garlic, twisting at top to make neat parcel. Place in oven for 45 minutes. Leave to cool, then squeeze garlic out of skins into small bowl. Mash garlic and stir in 30 ml (2 tbsp) oil, until smooth. To prepare hearth bread, place baking stone or tiles on middle rack and preheat oven to 200°C (400°F Gas Mark 6). Place flour, yeast, and salt in large bowl of standing mixer. Combine olive oil and warm water in measuring cup. Slowly incorporate tablespoons of oil mixture into flour, then change to dough hook attachment and knead for 5 to 6 minutes, until dough is smooth and elastic. Turn dough into lightly oiled bowl, cover with cling film, and place in warm spot to rise for 1 hour, or until doubled in size. Knock dough back once to deflate and turn onto lightly floured board or counter. Using sharp knife, divide dough in half. Using fingers or rolling pin, shape first piece into oblong shape, roughly 25 x 15 cm (10 x 6 in). With fingertips, dimple surface of dough, and spread half roasted garlic on each piece. Cover breads with a few overlapping damp paper towels and set aside for 20 minutes. Lightly flour pizza peel. Gently shake hearth breads, one at a time, onto baking stone or tiles. Bake for 20 minutes, until puffy and golden brown. Transfer to wire rack and cool for 20 minutes.

Makes 2. Serves 4–6.

poppy seed flatbread

see variations page 221

This pretty flatbread uses easy-blend dried yeast, which is fast acting, so the combined rising time is less than one hour.

375 g (13 oz) strong white bread flour
225 g (8 oz) plain flour
10 ml (2 tsp) easy-blend dried yeast
10 ml (2 tsp) salt
45 ml (3 tbsp) sugar

45 ml (3 tbsp) extra-virgin
  olive oil
500 ml (18 fl oz) warm water
30 ml (2 tbsp) milk
60 ml (4 tbsp) poppy seeds

In large bowl of standing mixer, combine 225 g (8 oz) of the flour with the yeast, salt and sugar. Combine oil and warm water. Pour oil mixture into flour mixture and combine slowly, until flour is moistened. Add remaining flour 50 g (2 oz) at a time. When all flour is incorporated, change to dough hook attachment and knead for 4 to 5 minutes, until dough is smooth and elastic. Cover bowl with cling film and place in warm spot to rise for 30 minutes. Preheat oven to 190°C (375°F / Gas Mark 5). Knock dough back once to deflate. Using sharp knife, cut dough in half.

Roll out each piece into an oblong shape, 2.5 cm (1 in) thick. Place each loaf on baking sheet lined with baking paper. Dimple surface of dough with fingers, cover with clean dish towels, and set aside for 15 minutes. Press dimples once more, brush top of each loaf with 15 ml (1 tbsp) milk, and sprinkle 30 ml (2 tbsp) poppy seeds on top. Bake for 25 to 30 minutes, until puffy and golden brown. Serve warm or at room temperature.

Makes 2. Serves 6–8.

variations

matzoh

see base recipe page 199

matzoh with sesame seeds
Prepare the basic recipe, spreading 115-225 g (4-8 oz) sesame seeds on a
clean board. Once matzoh has been rolled and cut, press both sides of piece
into seeds, until each piece is well covered. Shake off excess before baking.

matzoh with poppy seeds
Prepare the basic recipe, spreading 115-225 g (4-8 oz) poppy seeds on a
clean board. Once matzoh has been rolled and cut, press both sides of piece
into seeds, until each piece is well covered. Shake off excess before baking.

matzoh with honey
Prepare the basic recipe, spreading 15 ml (1 tbsp) honey on each piece
before serving.

matzoh with halvah
Prepare the basic recipe, topping each piece of matzoh with 1 to
2 slices halvah before serving.

matzoh with tahini
Prepare the basic recipe, spreading each piece with 15 ml (1 tbsp)
tahini before serving.

manakish

see base recipe page 200

manakish with feta
Prepare the basic recipe, topping manakish with 75 g (3 oz) crumbled
feta before baking.

manakish with tomato
Prepare the basic recipe, topping manakish with 1 small chopped tomato
before baking.

manakish with fresh mint leaves
Prepare the basic recipe, sprinkling baked manakish with 3 to 4 torn
fresh mint leaves.

manakish with black olives
Prepare the basic recipe, topping manakish with 50 g (2 oz) sliced black
olives before baking.

manakish with pickled turnip
Prepare the basic recipe, topping manakish with 75 g (3 oz) chopped
pickled turnip.

variations

sangak

see base recipe page 203

sangak with poppy seeds
Prepare the basic recipe, replacing the sesame seeds with an equal quantity
of poppy seeds.

sangak with nigella seeds
Prepare the basic recipe, replacing the sesame seeds with an equal
quantity of nigella seeds.

sangak with cumin seeds
Prepare the basic recipe, replacing the sesame seeds with 30 ml (2 tbsp)
cumin seeds. Sprinkle 2.5 ml (½ tsp) over each piece of sangak.

sangak with coriander seeds
Prepare the basic recipe, replacing the sesame seeds with 30 ml (2 tbsp)
coriander seeds. Sprinkle 2.5 ml (½ tsp) over each piece of sangak.

sangak with caraway seeds
Prepare the basic recipe, replacing the sesame seeds with 30 ml (2 tbsp)
caraway seeds. Sprinkle 2.5 ml (½ tsp) over each piece of sangak.

variations

barbari

see base recipe page 204

barbari with feta
Prepare the basic recipe, topping each barbari with 75 g (3 oz) crumbled
feta before baking.

barbari with nigella seeds
Prepare the basic recipe, replacing the sesame seeds with an equal quantity
of nigella seeds.

barbari with raisins
Prepare the basic recipe, adding 50 g (3 oz) raisins with the flour.

barbari with oats
Prepare the basic recipe, omitting sesame seeds. Sprinkle each barbari with
30 ml (2 tbsp) quick-cooking oats.

barbari with sunflower seeds
Prepare the basic recipe, replacing sesame seeds with an equal quantity
of sunflower seeds.

variations

pitta

see base recipe page 208

garlic pitta chips
Preheat oven 180°C (350°F / Gas Mark 4). Cut pitta into 6 equal wedges and place on large baking sheet. Coat each wedge with a thin film of extra-virgin olive oil and sprinkle with a pinch of garlic salt. Bake for 5 to 7 minutes, until crisp.

pitta with hummus
Prepare the basic recipe, topping each pitta with 30 ml (2 tbsp) hummus before serving.

pitta with tzatziki
Prepare the basic recipe, topping each pitta with 30 ml (2 tbsp) tzatziki before serving.

wholemeal pitta
Prepare the basic recipe, replacing the plain flour with an equal quantity of wholemeal flour.

pitta with pomegranate & mint yogurt dip
Prepare the basic recipe, topping each pitta with a dip made of 15 ml (1 tbsp) chopped fresh mint, 30 ml (2 tbsp) natural yogurt, and a pinch of salt.

lavash

see base recipe page 208

lavash with toasted sesame seeds
Prepare the basic recipe, adding 2.5 ml (½ tsp) toasted sesame seeds
to the dough with the flour.

lavash with poppy seeds
Prepare the basic recipe, adding 5 ml (1 tsp) poppy seeds to the dough
with the flour.

lavash with sunflower seeds
Prepare the basic recipe, adding 5 ml (1 tsp) chopped sunflower seeds
to the dough with the flour.

lavash with cumin seeds
Prepare the basic recipe, adding 2.5 ml (½ tsp) slightly crushed cumin
seeds to the dough with the flour.

lavash with ground sumac
Prepare the basic recipe, adding 2.5 ml (½ tsp) ground sumac to the dough
with the flour.

garlic hearth bread

see base recipe page 211

garlic & cheese hearth bread
Prepare the basic recipe, sprinkling 45 ml (3 tbsp) finely grated Parmesan over the roasted garlic mixture.

garlic & thyme hearth bread
Prepare the basic recipe, adding 1.25 ml (¼ tsp) dried and crumbled thyme to the roasted garlic mixture.

garlic & rosemary hearth bread
Prepare the basic recipe, adding 1.25 ml (¼ tsp) dried and crumbled rosemary to the roasted garlic mixture.

garlic & pink peppercorn hearth bread
Prepare the basic recipe, adding 5 ml (1 tsp) ground pink peppercorns to the dough just before changing to the dough hook attachment.

garlic & parsley hearth bread
Prepare the basic recipe, adding 60 ml (4 tbsp) chopped fresh flat-leaf parsley to the roasted garlic mixture.

poppy seed flatbread

see base recipe page 212

garlic & poppy seed flatbread
Prepare the basic recipe, sprinkling 1 crushed garlic clove over each flatbread with the poppy seeds.

celery & poppy seed flatbread
Prepare the basic recipe, sprinkling 1.25 ml (¼ tsp) celery seeds over each flatbread with the poppy seeds.

poppy seed flatbread with smoked paprika
Prepare the basic recipe, adding 1.25 ml (¼ tsp) smoked paprika to the dough just before changing to the dough hook attachment.

poppy seed flatbread with cumin
Prepare the basic recipe, adding 1.25 ml (¼ tsp) ground cumin to the dough just before changing to the dough hook attachment.

poppy seed flatbread with cardamom
Prepare the basic recipe, adding 1.25 ml (¼ tsp) ground cardamom to the dough just before changing to the dough hook attachment.

flatbreads of the americas

In the earliest settlements in all regions of the
Americas, people have taken grain, ground it, mixed
it with water and cooked it over fire. This chapter
contains the best of these enduring recipes.

wheat tortillas

see variations page 242

Used for making everything from burritos to quesadillas and wraps, this is one recipe you'll want to master.

250 g (9 oz) bread flour, preferably unbleached
5 ml (½ tsp) salt
45 ml (3 tbsp) corn oil
120 ml (4 fl oz) warm water

In large bowl of standing mixer, combine flour and salt. Slowly stir in oil. When oil is well incorporated, add warm water. Mix on slow speed until all flour is moistened and dough sticks together. Add up to 60 ml (4 tbsp) more water as necessary to get dough to hold. Change to dough hook and knead for 1 to 2 minutes. Turn dough onto lightly floured surface and divide into 8 equal portions. Shape pieces into 8-cm (3-in) discs, place on baking sheet, and cover with cling film. Set aside for 30 minutes.

Using a tortilla press or a rolling pin, roll out rounds to form 20-cm (8-in) tortillas. Preheat large cast-iron or nonstick frying pan over medium heat.

Place first tortilla in hot frying pan and cook for less than 1 minute per side, or until brown spots appear. Repeat with remaining dough. Stack cooked tortillas and keep warm in tortilla basket or wrapped in a clean paper towel.

Makes 8. Serves 3–4.

masa harina tortillas

see variations page 243

In Mexico, corn is soaked in a water and quicklime mixture to soften the grain and help remove the husks before it is ground into flour for corn tortillas. To skip this step, buy prepared masa harina from a deli or on-line supplier. This type of flour has been developed specifically for tortillas.

275 g (10 oz) masa harina
300 ml (½ pint) hot water

In large bowl of standing mixer, combine masa harina and hot water. Mix on slow speed until all flour is moistened and dough sticks together. Add more water or flour as necessary to get a soft dough that is not sticky.

Change to dough hook and knead for 1 to 2 minutes. Turn dough onto lightly floured surface and divide into 16 equal portions. Shape each piece into a ball and flatten into a 5-cm (2-in) round.

Using a tortilla press or a rolling pin, roll out rounds to form 15-cm (6-in) tortillas. Preheat large cast-iron or nonstick frying pan over medium heat.

Place first tortilla in hot frying pan and cook for less than 1 minute per side, or until brown spots appear. Repeat with remaining dough. Stack cooked tortillas and keep warm in tortilla basket or wrapped in a clean paper towel.

Makes 16. Serves 6–8.

bannock

see variations page 244

Bannock originated in Scotland and were introduced to the United States by early settlers. They can be cooked in a cast-iron frying pan over a campfire, or even wrapped around a stick and held 20 cm (8 in) above the flames until cooked.

115 g (4 oz) plain flour
5 ml (1 tsp) baking powder
4 ml (³/₄ tbsp) salt
45 ml (3 tbsp) unsalted butter
120 ml (4 fl oz) water

In large bowl, combine flour, baking powder and salt. Cut in the butter until the mixture resembles a coarse meal. Add 120 ml (4 fl oz) water and stir until flour is moistened and a stiff dough forms. Add more water if necessary.

Lightly oil and preheat a large cast-iron or nonstick frying pan over medium heat.

Turn dough onto lightly floured board or counter. Divide into 4 equal pieces. Flatten each piece to form a round that is 1 cm (¹/₂ in) thick.

Place first round in hot frying pan and cook for 6 to 7 minutes per side. Serve warm with butter or desired topping. Cook remaining pieces of bannock in the same way.

Makes 4. Serves 2–4.

pan fry bread

see variations page 245

This deep-fried Navajo bread is often served at powwows and First Nations gatherings around North America.

350 g (12 oz) plain flour, preferably unbleached
15 ml (1 tbsp) baking powder
pinch of bicarbonate of soda
5 ml (1 tsp) salt

175 ml (6 fl oz) creamy milk
175 ml (6 fl oz) hot water
15 ml (1 tbsp) rapeseed oil, plus more for
    deep-frying

In large bowl of standing mixer, combine flour, baking powder, bicarbonate of soda and salt. Combine milk and hot water and stir into flour mixture.

Change to dough hook attachment and knead for 2 to 3 minutes, until you have a smooth dough. Turn dough into oiled bowl, rolling dough so it is covered in a light oil film. Cover bowl with cling film and set aside for 30 minutes.

Turn dough onto lightly floured board or counter. Divide dough into 10 equal pieces. Shape pieces into balls and flatten each ball to form a round, 12 cm (5 in) wide and 5 mm (⅛ in) thick.

Deep-fry pieces of dough in pan of 5 cm (2 in) deep hot oil for 1 minute per side, until golden brown. Transfer fry bread to paper towel to drain. Serve warm.

Makes 10. Serves 4–5.

gorditas

see variations page 246

Gorditas are the stuffed flatbreads popular in the Durango region of Mexico. The name accurately translates into "little fat ones!"

150 g (5 oz) masa harina
2.5 ml (1½ tsp) salt
2.5 ml (1½ tsp) baking powder
30 ml (2 tbsp) plain flour
225 ml (8 fl oz) warm water
225 g (8 oz) lean minced beef

½ mild onion, finely chopped
freshly ground black pepper
pinch of chilli powder
175 g (6 oz) grated Monterey
    Jack or cheddar cheese
rapeseed oil for deep-frying

In large bowl of standing mixer, combine masa harina, ½ teaspoon salt, baking powder and plain flour. Add warm water and mix on slow speed until all flour is moistened and dough sticks together. Add more water or flour as necessary to get a soft dough that is not sticky. Change to dough hook and knead for 1 to 2 minutes. Cover bowl with cling film and set aside for 30 minutes. To prepare filling, brown the beef and onions over medium heat in a large, cast-iron frying pan until meat is cooked through and onions have softened and are beginning to brown, 4 to 5 minutes. Stir in remaining ingredients except cheese and set aside. Preheat oven to 180°C (350°F / Gas Mark 4). Turn dough onto lightly floured surface. Divide dough into 6 equal pieces. Roll pieces into balls, then flatten each into a 6-cm (2½-in) round which is 5 mm. (¼ in) thick. Keeping the remaining pieces covered to prevent drying, deep-fry rounds in hot oil, 5 cm (2 in) deep. Cook for less than 1 minute per side, and

continuously spoon hot oil over the top. When the gordita is puffy and golden brown, use tongs to transfer it to a paper towel to drain. Cook the remaining gorditas in the same way. Use a sharp bread knife to slice gordita in half horizontally. Spread about 75 ml (5 tbsp) filling over the bottom half of each and replace the lid and sprinkle with the grated cheese. Place stuffed gorditas on ovenproof plate and place in a pre-heated oven to keep warm.

Makes 6. Serves 2–3.

arepas

see variations page 247

Arepas are a Venezuelan specialty, common at food stalls and cooked at home.
Eat them plain, as an alternative to bread rolls, or fill them and serve as a sandwich.

275 g (10 oz) masa harina
2.5 ml (1/2 tsp) salt
580 ml (scant 1 pint) warm water
30 ml (2 tbsp) rapeseed oil

Preheat oven to 200°C (400°F / Gas Mark 6). In large bowl of standing mixer, combine masa harina and salt. Add hot water and mix on slow speed until all flour is moistened and dough sticks together. Leave to stand for 5 minutes.

Change to dough hook and knead for 1 to 2 minutes. Turn dough onto lightly floured surface. Divide dough into 8 equal pieces. Roll pieces into balls, then flatten into 7.5-cm (3-in) round that is 2-cm (3/4-in) thick. Preheat oil in large frying pan.

Working with one or two pieces at a time and keeping the remaining pieces covered to prevent drying, fry rounds for 3 to 4 minute per side, flipping 3 to 4 times, until crisp and golden brown. Transfer arepas to paper towel to drain. Repeat with remaining pieces.

Place fried arepas on baking sheet and bake in the preheated oven for 15 minutes. Serve warm or at room temperature.

Makes 8. Serves 3–4.

jamaican bammy bread

see variations page 248

This Jamaican speciality is soaked in coconut milk before being fried a second time. It is traditionally enjoyed with fried fish.

2 large cassavas (yuca), total weight about
    450 g (1 lb)
pinch of salt
40 g (1½ oz) unsalted butter
225 ml (8 fl oz) coconut milk

Peel and finely grate cassavas. Wrap in a clean paper towel and press over the sink to remove as much moisture as possible. Add salt and divide into three portions.

Flatten portion to form a round or bammy 15 cm (6 in) in diameter and 1 cm (½ in) thick. Heat 15 g (½ oz) butter in frying pan. Once butter has melted, place first round in frying pan and cook over medium heat for 9 to 10 minutes. Flip bammy and cook on other side for 9 to 10 minutes.

Remove bammy and place in shallow dish. Pour over coconut milk and leave to soak for 5 to 10 minutes.

Return bammy to frying pan and cook over medium heat for 3 to 4 minutes per side, until each side is golden brown. Cook the other bammies in the same way.

Makes 3. Serves 3 to 6

cornbread

see variations page 249

Cornbread is a popular bread enjoyed all over the Americas. It is easy to make and satisfying with chilli or other spicy stews.

40 g (1½ oz) vegetable fat, lard or bacon drippings
2 large eggs
215 g (7½ oz) cornmeal

5 ml (1 tsp) salt
2.5 ml (½ tsp) bicarbonate of soda
300 ml (½ pint) buttermilk

Preheat oven to 200°C (400°F / Gas Mark 6). If baking cornbread in 25-cm (10-in) cast-iron frying pan with an ovenproof handle. Otherwise, melt fat and place in a large rectangular baking dish, 33 x 23-cm (13 x 9-in).

Place eggs in large bowl of standing mixer. Beat on medium-high speed until frothy. Stir in cornmeal, salt, and bicarbonate of soda until well incorporated. Stir in buttermilk until it forms a smooth batter.

Tilt frying pan to make sure surface is thoroughly greased, then pour any surplus remaining fat into the batter. Stir to blend.

Pour batter into the frying pan or dish and bake for 25 to 30 minutes, until cornbread is firm and pulling away from sides of the pan or dish. Slice into wedges and serve hot.

Makes 1. Serves 6–8.

sope

see variations page 250

Sope is a Mexican corn patty that can be topped with any number of savory fillings.

425 g (15 oz) masa harina
150 g (5 oz) sweetcorn, canned or frozen
115 g (4 oz) vegetable fat, softened

45 ml (3 tbsp) water
1.25 ml (¼ tsp) salt
freshly ground white pepper

In large bowl of standing mixer, combine masa harina, corn, vegetable fat, water, and salt. Mix with paddle attachment until dough comes together. Add more water if necessary so that dough holds together.

Change to dough hook attachment and knead for 3 to 4 minutes, until dough is smooth. Turn dough onto lightly floured board or counter. Using lightly floured rolling pin, roll dough out to a thickness of 2.5 cm (1 in). Cut rounds (sopes) with a 10-cm (4-in) scone or biscuit cutter.

Preheat large cast-iron or non-stick frying pan over medium heat. Cook sopes one at a time for 3 minutes each side.

Transfer to paper towel to drain. Season with white pepper.

Repeat until all sopes are cooked. If serving warm, place sopes on lightly greased baking sheet and place in preheated 275°F (140°C) oven until ready to serve.

Makes 12. Serves 6–8.

pupusa

see variations page 251

Pupusas are stuffed corn flatbreads that originate from El Salvador, where they are served with hot sauce and curtido, a condiment similar to coleslaw.

700 g (1 lb 9 oz) masa harina
1 litre (1³/₄ pints) water
1 x 397 g (14 oz) can refried beans
350 g (12 oz) grated mozzarella
extra-virgin olive oil

In large bowl of standing mixer, combine masa harina and water until all flour is incorporated and a dough forms. Turn onto a lightly floured board or counter and divide dough into 25 equal pieces. Roll each piece into a ball and flatten into a 1-cm (¹/₂-in) thick round. Place about 15 ml (1 tbsp) refried beans and 30 ml (2 tbsp) grated mozzarella in the middle of the round, fold over, and flatten once more so that filling is completely enclosed in dough.

Brush large cast-iron or nonstick frying pan with extra-virgin olive oil and preheat over medium heat. Cook pupusas one at a time for 4 to 5 minutes per side, until firm and golden brown. Transfer to paper towels to drain. Repeat until all pupusas are cooked.

Place cooked pupusas on lightly greased baking sheet and keep warm in preheated 140°C (275°F / Gas Mark 1) oven until ready to serve.

Makes 25. Serves 8–10.

wheat tortillas

see base recipe page 223

herb tortillas
Prepare the basic recipe, adding 2.5 ml (½ tsp) Italian seasoning.

sun-dried tomato tortillas
Prepare the basic recipe, adding a 15 ml (1 tbsp) package of sun-dried tomato pesto to the flour mixture.

wholemeal tortillas
Prepare the basic recipe, replacing 150 g (5 oz) bread flour with 150 g (5 oz) wholemeal flour.

wheat tortilla chips
Prepare the basic recipe. Once the tortillas have completely cooled, cut each tortilla in half, and each half in fourths, so that you have 8 equal wedges. Preheat oven to 180°C (350°F / Gas Mark 4). Place wedges in a single layer on large baking sheet and bake for 10 to 12 minutes, until golden brown.

spicy tortilla chips
Prepare the basic recipe. Once the tortillas have cooled, cut each tortilla into 8 wedges. Preheat oven to 180°C (350°F / Gas Mark 4). Place wedges in single layer on baking sheet, brush with olive oil, and sprinkle with a pinch of BBQ or Cajun seasoning. Bake for 10 to 12 minutes, until golden brown.

variations

masa harina tortillas

see base recipe page 224

masa harina tortilla chips
Prepare the basic recipe. Once the tortillas have completely cooled, cut
each tortilla in half, and each half in fourths, so that you have 8 equal
wedges. Preheat oven to 180°C (350°F / Gas Mark 4). Place tortilla wedges in
single layer on large baking sheet, and bake for 10 to 12 minutes, until
golden brown.

masa harina tortillas with chili pepper
Prepare the basic recipe, adding a pinch of crushed red pepper flakes
to the masa harina mixture.

masa harina tortillas with mixed peppercorns
Prepare the basic recipe, adding 1.25 ml (¼ tsp) freshly ground mixed
peppercorns to the masa harina mixture.

blue corn tortillas
Prepare the basic recipe, replacing the masa harina with 150 g (5 oz) blue
cornmeal and 115 g (4 oz) plain flour.

variations

bannock

see base recipe page 227

bannock with blueberries
Prepare the basic recipe, folding 25 g (1 oz) fresh blueberries into the dough.

bannock with raisins
Prepare the basic recipe, folding 40 g (1½ oz) raisins into the dough.

bannock with cranberries
Prepare the basic recipe, folding 25 g (1 oz) fresh or frozen cranberries into the dough.

cinnamon bannock
Prepare the basic recipe, adding 1.25 ml (¼ tsp) ground cinnamon with the flour.

pan fry bread

see base recipe page 228

pan fry bread with wild blueberry jam
Prepare the basic recipe, topping each fry bread with 30 ml (2 tbsp)
wild blueberry jam before serving.

pan fry bread with maple syrup
Prepare the basic recipe, drizzling 15 ml (1 tbsp) maple syrup over each
piece of fry bread before serving.

pan fry bread with fresh tomato salsa
Prepare the basic recipe, topping each fry bread with 30 ml (2 tbsp)
fresh tomato salsa before serving.

pan fry bread with sugar & lemon juice
Prepare the basic recipe, topping each piece of fry bread with 5 ml (1 tsp)
granulated sugar and 2.5 ml (½ tsp) fresh lemon juice before serving.

variations

gorditas

see base recipe page 230

wholemeal gorditas
Prepare the basic recipe, replacing 65 g (2½ oz) masa harina with ½ cup wholemeal flour.

gorditas stuffed with prickly pear
Prepare the basic recipe, replacing the beef filling with 60 ml (4 tbsp) prickly pear (*nopales*) salsa.

gorditas with chicken
Prepare the basic recipe, replacing the beef filling with 60 ml (4 tbsp) shredded cooked chicken and 15 ml (1 tbsp) tomato salsa.

gorditas with green salsa
Prepare the basic recipe, adding 15 ml (1 tbsp) green salsa to teach gordita with the beef filling.

arepas

see base recipe page 233

blue corn flour arepas
Prepare the basic recipe, replacing the masa harina with 150 g (5 oz) blue cornmeal and 115 g (4 oz) plain flour.

arepas stuffed with scrambled egg
Prepare the basic recipe, slicing each arepa in half horizontally and filling with 30-45 ml (2-3 tbsp) scrambled eggs.

wholemeal arepas
Prepare the basic recipe, replacing 150 g (5 oz) masa harina with 125 g (4 ½ oz) wholemeal flour.

coconut arepas
Prepare the basic recipe, adding about 45 ml (3 tbsp) shredded coconut to the masa harina mixture.

variations

jamaican bammy bread

see base recipe page 234

potato bammy bread
Prepare the basic recipe, replacing 175 g (6 oz) grated cassava with the same quantiy of finely grated potato.

sweet potato bammy bread
Prepare the basic recipe, replacing 175 g (6 oz) grated cassava with the same quantity of finely grated sweet potato.

beetroot & cassava bammy bread
Prepare the basic recipe, replacing 175 g (6 oz) grated cassava with the same quantity of finely grated beetroot.

carrot & cassava bammy bread
Prepare the basic recipe, replacing 175 g (6 oz) grated cassava with the same quantity of finely grated carrot.

variations

cornbread

see base recipe page 237

cornbread with cayenne pepper
Prepare the basic recipe, adding a pinch of cayenne pepper with
the cornmeal.

cornbread with sweet red pepper
Prepare the basic recipe, adding ½ large red pepper, diced, with
the cornmeal.

corn & cheese bread
Prepare the basic recipe, adding 40 g (1½ oz) grated cheddar or Monterey
Jack cheese to the batter with the cornmeal. Sprinkle 25 g (1 oz) grated
cheese on top of batter before baking.

cornbread with dill
Prepare the basic recipe, adding 5 ml (1 tsp) dried or 15 ml (1 tbsp) chopped
fresh dill to the batter with the cornmeal.

variations

sope

see base recipe page 238

sope with chilli pepper
Prepare the basic recipe, adding 2.5 ml (½ tsp) crushed red pepper flakes to the dough with the masa harina.

sope with guacamole
Prepare the basic recipe, topping each sope with 60 ml (4 tbsp) guacamole and 2 to 3 leaves fresh coriander before serving.

sope with shredded pork
Prepare the basic recipe, topping each sope with 45 ml (3 tbsp) shredded cooked pork and 30 ml (2 tbsp) tomato salsa before serving.

sope with green olives
Prepare the basic recipe, topping each sope with 30 ml (2 tbsp) sliced green olives before serving.

sope with chicken
Prepare the basic recipe, topping each sope with 45 ml (3 tbsp) shredded cooked chicken and 30 ml (2 tbsp) tomato salsa before serving.

variations

pupusa

see base recipe page 241

rice pupusa
Prepare the basic recipe, replacing 150 g (5 oz) masa harina with an equal quantity of rice flour.

pupusa filled with chicharron
Prepare the basic recipe, replacing the refried bean filling with chicharron. To prepare the chicharron, slice 450 g (1 lb) pork skin into 5-cm (2-in) slices and sprinkle with salt. Cover and place in refrigerator for 1 hour. Fry pork slices for 5 to 6 minutes, until crispy. Drain on paper towels.

pupusa filled with green salsa
Prepare the basic recipe, topping each pupusa with 15 ml (1 tbsp) green salsa.

pupusa stuffed with cheese and herbs
Prepare the basic recipe, omitting refried beans. Add 15 ml (1 tbsp) finely chopped fresh coriander to each pupusa with the grated mozzarella.

sweet pizzas & flatbreads

When you are craving something sweet

and a little different, try one of these

scrumptious treats.

chocolate pizza

see variations page 272

This dessert is easy to assemble and always a big hit with chocolate lovers.

1/3 recipe basic thin pizza base
   (page 17)
10 ml (2 tsp) unsalted butter, melted

75 ml (5 tbsp) prepared chocolate sauce
40 g (1½ oz) white chocolate chips
40 g (1½ oz) milk chocolate chips

Place pizza stone on bottom rack of oven and preheat to 230°C (450°F / Gas Mark 8). Roll pizza dough out to a 25-cm (10-in) round.

Lightly flour a pizza peel. Place the pizza base on the peel, dimple the surface with fingertips and glaze with unsalted butter. Gently shake the pizza from the peel onto baking stone.

Bake for 15 to 20 minutes, until base is slightly puffy and golden brown.

Remove the base from the oven. Spread chocolate sauce over pizza base, sprinkle chocolate chips over the sauce, then return it to the oven for 1 to 2 minutes, until the chocolate chips begin to melt.

Transfer to a wire rack to cool. Serve warm or at room temperature.

Makes one 25-cm (10-in) pizza. Serves 4–6.

apple cranberry pizza

see variations page 273

It is not surprising to find that fruit makes a tempting topping for pizzas!

⅓ recipe basic thin pizza base (page 17)
50 g (2 oz) dried cranberries
4 medium apples, peeled, cored, and finely
    chopped

45 ml (3 tbsp) brown sugar
25 g (1 oz) unsalted butter, melted
10 ml (2 tsp) freshly squeezed lemon juice
5 ml (1 tsp) ground cinnamon

Place a pizza stone on middle rack of oven and preheat to 230°C (450°F / Gas Mark 8). Roll pizza dough out to a 30-cm (12-in) round. Lightly flour pizza peel.

Place pizza base on peel, and sprinkle with dried cranberries. In a medium bowl, combine chopped apple, sugar, butter, lemon juice and cinnamon.

Spread apple mixture over cranberries. Gently shake pizza from peel onto baking stone.

Bake for 15 to 20 minutes, until base is slightly puffy and golden brown.

Remove the pizza from the oven and transfer to wire rack to cool. Serve warm or at room temperature.

Makes one 30-cm (12-in) pizza. Serves 4–6.

streusel pizza

see variations page 274

This luscious pizza is topped with a cream cheese mixture, fresh berries and a crumbly topping.

$^1/_3$ recipe basic thin pizza base (page 17)
topping
115 g (4 oz) cream cheese, softened
1 large egg yolk
1.25 ml ($^1/_4$ tsp) vanilla essence
7.5 ml ($1^1/_2$ tsp) sugar
75 g (3 oz) fresh strawberries, hulled

streusel
60 g ($2^1/_2$ oz) light brown sugar
25 g (3 oz) unsalted butter, melted
15 ml (1 tbsp) plain flour

Preheat oven to 200°C (400°F / Gas Mark 6).

Line a 30-cm (12-in) pizza pan with baking paper. Roll pizza dough out to a 30-cm (12-in) round and place in pan. In medium bowl, combine cream cheese, egg yolk, vanilla and sugar. Stir until smooth.

In small bowl, combine all the streusel ingredients until you have a crumbly mixture. Spread the cream cheese mixture over the pizza base, top with strawberries and sprinkle with streusel.

Place on middle rack of preheated oven and bake for 25 to 30 minutes, until the base is baked and the streusel topping is crunchy. Serve warm or at room temperature.

Makes one 30-cm (12-in) pizza. Serves 4–6.

vanilla flatbread

see variations page 275

This gently scented flatbread pairs perfectly with a cup of tea or a café au lait.

dough
12.5 ml (2 1/2 tsp) active
    dried yeast
50 g (2 oz) plus 2.5 ml ($^1/_2$
    tsp) sugar
120 ml (4 fl oz) warm water
300 g (10$^1/_2$ oz) plain flour
75 ml (5 tbsp) whole milk

pinch of salt
20 ml (4 tsp) vanilla essence
1 vanilla pod
3 large eggs
115 g (4 oz) unsalted butter,
    softened and cut into
    8 pieces

glaze
40 g (1$^1/_2$ tbsp) unsalted
    butter, melted
5 ml (1 tsp) vanilla essence
50 g (2 oz) demerara sugar

To prepare the dough, sprinkle yeast and 2.5 ml ($^1/_2$ tsp) sugar over warm water in medium bowl. Set aside for 5 minutes, until foamy. Add 40 g (1$^1/_2$ oz) of the flour and stir until mixture is smooth. Cover with cling film and set aside for 30 minutes. Slowly heat milk in medium saucepan over low heat. Stir in the remaining sugar and salt. Remove from heat and cool for 2 to 3 minutes. Pour milk mixture into large bowl of standing mixer. Add vanilla essence. Slit the vanilla pod and scrape the seeds into the milk mixture, then add the eggs and blend on slow speed until well mixed. Blend in yeast mixture, then add flour 75 g (3 oz) at a time. Add the butter, one piece at a time. Change to dough hook and knead for 4 to 5 minutes until dough is smooth, elastic, and sticky. Turn dough into lightly greased bowl, cover with cling film, and place in a warm spot to rise for 1$^1/_2$ to 2 hours, until doubled in volume. Cover 2 large rectangular baking sheets with baking paper. Turn dough onto lightly floured surface. Using a sharp knife, cut dough in half. Shape each piece into an oblong,

roughly 20-23 cm (8-9 in) long shape. Place on baking sheets, cover with a clean paper towel, and return to warm spot to rise for 1 additional hour. Preheat oven to 190°C (375°F / Gas Mark 5). To prepare the glaze, combine melted butter and vanilla essence. Glaze the surfaces of both flatbreads, then sprinkle each with 30 ml (2 tbsp) demerara sugar. Bake flatbreads for 25 minutes, until tops are golden brown. Transfer to wire rack to cool. Serve warm or at room temperature.

Makes 2. Serves 6–8.

sweet fried flatbread

see variations page 276

Similar in taste and texture to sugar doughnuts, this cinnamon-dusted fried flatbread is sure to please.

75 ml (5 tbsp) sugar
120 ml (4 fl oz) warm water
25 ml (5 tsp) active dried yeast
pinch of sugar
225 ml (8 fl oz) warm milk
5 ml (1 tsp) vanilla essence
2 large eggs

75 ml (5 tbsp) rapeseed oil
450-550 g (16-20 oz) plain flour
75 ml (5 tbsp) salt
rapeseed oil for frying

topping
225 g (8 oz) sugar

In large bowl of standing mixer, sprinkle yeast and pinch of sugar over warm water. Set aside for 5 minutes, until yeast becomes foamy. With paddle attachment, stir in remaining sugar, milk, vanilla, eggs and oil. Stir in 450 g (1 lb) of the flour and the salt. Add more flour as necessary to form a soft dough. With dough hook, knead for 4 to 5 minutes, until dough is smooth and elastic. Cover bowl with cling film and set aside for 1 hour. Turn dough onto lightly floured board to deflate. Using sharp knife, divide dough into 22 to 24 equal egg-sized pieces. Shape each piece into a ball. Using rolling pin or fingers, stretch out each ball to form a 15-cm (6-in) oval, 3 mm (⅛ in) thick. Keep rolled-out pieces covered while you prepare remaining ones. Deep-fry pieces of dough in hot oil 5-cm (2-in) for 1 minute per side, until dark golden brown. Remove with tongs and transfer to paper towels to drain. Place sugar for the topping in a large bowl. Toss flatbread in sugar, shaking off excess as you pull them out of the bowl. Serve warm.

Makes 22–24. Serves 10–12.

lemon & cranberry flatbread

see variations page 277

This is a wonderfully fun and deliciously tart flatbread.

12.5 ml (2½ tsp) active dried yeast
50 g (2 oz) plus 2.5 ml (½ tsp) sugar
120 ml (½ cup) warm water
300 g (10½ oz) plain flour
75 ml (5 tbsp) creamy milk
pinch of salt
3 large eggs

300 g (10½ oz) plain flour
115 g (4 oz) unsalted butter, softened and
    cut into 8 pieces
grated rind and juice of 1 large lemon
50 g (2 oz) dried cranberries

To prepare dough, sprinkle the yeast and 2.5 ml (½ tsp) sugar over warm water in medium bowl. Set aside for 5 minutes, until foamy. Add 40 g (1½ oz) of the flour and stir until smooth. Cover with cling film and set aside for 30 minutes. Heat milk in medium saucepan over low heat. Stir in the remaining sugar and the salt. Remove from the heat and cool for 2 to 3 minutes. Pour milk mixture into large bowl of standing mixer. Add eggs and mix on slow speed until blended. Stir in yeast mixture, then add flour 75 g (3 oz) at a time. Add butter, one piece at a time. Stir in grated lemon rind, juice and cranberries. Change to dough hook and knead for 4 to 5 minutes until dough is smooth, elastic, and sticky. Turn dough into lightly greased bowl, cover with cling film, and place in warm spot to rise for 1½ to 2 hours, until doubled in volume. Cover 2 large rectangular baking sheets with baking paper. Turn dough onto lightly floured surface. Using sharp knife, cut dough in half. Shape each piece into an oblong, roughly 20–23 cm (8–9 in) long. Place on baking sheets, cover with paper towel, and return to warm spot to rise for 1 additional hour. Preheat oven to 190°C (375°F / Gas Mark 5) and bake flatbreads for 25 minutes, until tops are golden brown.

Makes 2. Serves 6–8.

ice cream pizza with brownie base

see variations page 278

The ultimate way to reward someone who has earned a lot of brownie points!

base
50 g (2 oz) plain flour
2.5 ml (¹/₂ tsp) baking powder
2.5 ml (¹/₂ tsp) salt
50 g (2 oz) unsalted butter
    75 g (3 oz) dark chocolate
    with 70 percent cocoa

solids, roughly chopped
225 g (8 oz) sugar
2 large eggs, lightly beaten
5 ml (1 tsp) vanilla essence
toppings
500 ml (18 fl oz) whipping
    cream

15 ml (1 tbsp) icing sugar
500 ml (18 fl oz) vanilla ice
    cream
60 ml (4 tbsp) assorted
    sweets for decoration

Preheat oven to 180°C (350°F / Gas Mark 4). Line a 30-cm (12-in) pizza pan that is about 1 cm (¹/₂ in) deep with baking paper. In a small bowl, combine flour, baking powder, and salt. In a double boiler, melt butter and chocolate until smooth. Remove from heat. Stir in sugar, eggs, and vanilla essence. Add flour mixture and stir until just combined. Spread brownie batter over baking paper in pizza pan. Bake on middle rack in oven for 13 to 15 minutes, until surface does not retain its indentation when touched. Transfer to wire rack and cool to room temperature. Transfer pan to refrigerator to cool for 30 minutes. Using standing mixer, beat whipping cream and confectioners' sugar until stiff peaks form. Remove ice cream from freezer and set aside for 5 minutes to soften slightly. Remove the brownie base from the refrigerator. Spread the softened ice cream in a 1-cm (¹/₂-in) layer over the brownie layer, leaving a 5-mm (¹/₄-in) border all round. Decorate with dollops of whipped cream and sweets. Transfer pizza to freezer until ready to serve.

Makes one 30-cm (12-in) pizza. Serves 4–6.

chocolate chip cookie base pizza

see variations page 279

If you ever have a group of children you really want to impress, try out this decadent dessert.

base
225 g (8 oz) plain flour
5 ml (1 tsp) bicarbonate of
    soda
2.5 ml (½ tsp) salt
175 g (6 oz) unsalted butter,
    softened

250 g (9 oz) light brown
    sugar
1 large egg, lightly beaten
10 ml (2 tsp) vanilla essence
215 g (7½ oz) chocolate chips

topping
350 ml (12 fl oz) ready-made
    vanilla frosting
75 ml (5 tbsp) prepared
    butterscotch or banoffee
    sauce

Preheat oven to 180°C (350°F / Gas Mark 4). In medium bowl, combine flour, baking soda, and salt. Set aside.

In large bowl of standing mixer, beat butter and brown sugar for 2 minutes, or until light and fluffy. Stir in egg and vanilla essence until well blended. Add flour mixture and stir just until it is incorporated. Stir in chocolate chips.

Line a 30-cm (12-in) pizza pan with baking paper. Turn dough onto pan and press down until pan is covered and top is smooth. Bake for 30 to 35 minutes, until top is golden brown and edges are a deeper brown. Transfer to wire rack to cool. Spread the frosting over the base and drizzle with butterscotch sauce.

Makes one 30-cm (12-in) pizza. Serves 6–8.

raspberry almond pizza

see variations page 280

This mouthwatering creation features a spectacular blend of marzipan and meringue in the topping.

²/₃ recipe basic thin pizza base (page 17)
3 large egg whites
115 g (4 oz) marzipan, softened
350 g (12 oz) seedless raspberry jam

215 g (7¹/₂ oz) fresh raspberries
150 g (5 oz) flaked almonds, toasted
30 ml (2 tbsp) icing sugar

Preheat oven to 230°C (450°F / Gas Mark 8). Line two 30-cm (12-in) pizza pans with baking paper. Roll pizza dough out to two 30-cm (12-in) round discs and place in pans.

In large bowl of standing mixer, beat egg whites until foamy. Add marzipan and stir until smooth. Fold in raspberry jam until fully incorporated.

Spread half the marzipan mixture over each pizza base, leaving a 1-cm (¹/₂-in) border.

Place on middle rack of preheated oven and bake for 10–12 minutes, until base is golden brown and topping is firm. Transfer to wire rack to cool.

Sprinkle each pizza with half the raspberries, almonds and icing sugar. Serve immediately.

Makes two 30-cm (12-in) pizzas. Serves 10–12.

fig, ricotta & honey pizza

see variations page 281

This delightful breakfast combination makes an elegant dessert pizza.

²/₃ recipe basic thin pizza base (page 17)
115 g (4 oz) ricotta
30 ml (2 tbsp) icing sugar

4–6 ripe figs, sliced lengthwise
45 ml (3 tbsp) clear honey

Place pizza stone on middle rack of oven and preheat to 230°C (450°F / Gas Mark 8). Roll pizza dough out to two 30-cm (12-in) rounds. Lightly flour a pizza peel. Place first pizza round on peel.

In large bowl of standing mixer, combine ricotta and sugar until smooth. Spread half the ricotta mixture over the pizza round, leaving a 1-cm (¹/₂-in) border. Arrange half the fig slices and drizzle half the honey on the pizza. Gently shake pizza from peel onto baking stone.

Bake for 12 to 15 minutes, until base is slightly puffy and golden brown.

Remove the pizza from the oven and transfer it to wire rack to cool. Repeat with second pizza.

Makes two 30-cm (12-in) pizzas. Serves 10–12.

variations

chocolate pizza

see base recipe page 253

chocolate hazelnut pizza
Prepare the basic recipe, replacing the prepared chocolate sauce with
an equal quantity of prepared chocolate-hazelnut spread.

chocolate raspberry pizza
Prepare the basic recipe, adding 30-45 ml (2-3 tbsp) fresh raspberries over
melted chocolate chips once the pizza has been removed from the oven for
the second time.

chocolate orange pizza
Prepare the basic recipe, replacing the milk chocolate chips with
an equal quantity of chopped orange-flavoured chocolate.

chocolate ginger pizza
Prepare the basic recipe, adding 30 ml (2 tbsp) chopped preserved stem
ginger over melted chocolate chips once the pizza has been removed from
the oven for the second time.

apple cranberry pizza

see base recipe page 254

apple cranberry pizza with coconut
Prepare the basic recipe, adding 20 g (³/₄ oz) desiccated coconut to the apple mixture.

apple cranberry pizza with almonds
Prepare the basic recipe, sprinkling 25 g (1 oz) flaked almonds over the apple mixture.

apple raisin pizza
Prepare the basic recipe, replacing the dried cranberries with an equal quantity of raisins.

cardamom apple pizza
Prepare the basic recipe, adding 1.25 ml (¹/₄ tsp) ground cardamom to the apple mixture.

variations

streusel pizza

see base recipe page 257

ricotta streusel pizza
Prepare the basic recipe, replacing the cream cheese with an equal quantity of ricotta.

marscapone streusel pizza
Prepare the basic recipe, replacing the cream cheese with an equal quantity of mascarpone.

streusel pizza with raspberries
Prepare the basic recipe, replacing the strawberries with an equal quantity of fresh raspberries.

streusel pizza with mixed berries
Prepare the basic recipe, replacing the strawberries with an equal quantity of assorted fresh berries.

variations

vanilla flatbread

see base recipe page 258

cinnamon flatbread
Prepare the basic recipe, replacing the vanilla essence and seeds with
2.5 ml (½ tsp) ground cinnamon. Replace vanilla essence in glaze
with 1.25 ml (¼ tsp) ground cinnamon.

vanilla cranberry flatbread
Prepare the basic recipe, adding 75 g (3 oz) dried cranberries to the dough
once all the flour has been incorporated.

carob flatbread
Prepare the basic recipe, omitting vanilla essence and seeds and adding
25 g (1 oz) carob powder with the flour. Omit vanilla glaze.

chocolate chip flatbread
Prepare the basic recipe, adding 75 g (3 oz) semisweet chocolate chips
to the dough once all the flour has been incorporated.

variations

sweet fried flatbread

see base recipe page 261

sweet fried flatbread with cinnamon sugar
Prepare the basic recipe, adding 2.5 ml (½ tsp) ground cinnamon
to the sugar topping.

sweet fried flatbread with apple compote
Prepare the basic recipe, topping each piece with 30 ml (2 tbsp) prepared
apple compote.

sweet fried flatbread with chocolate hazelnut spread
Prepare the basic recipe, omitting sugar topping. Top each piece with
30 ml (2 tbsp) chocolate hazelnut spread.

sweet fried flatbread with toasted pecans
Prepare the basic recipe, adding 40 g (1½ oz) finely chopped candied pecans
to the dough once the flour has been fully incorporated.

variations

lemon & cranberry flatbread

see base recipe page 262

lemon & blueberry flatbread
Prepare the basic recipe, replacing the dried cranberries with an equal
amount of dried blueberries.

lemon & currant flatbread
Prepare the basic recipe, replacing the dried cranberries with
an equal quantity of dried currants.

lemon & cherry flatbread
Prepare the basic recipe, replacing the dried cranberries with an equal
quantity of dried cherries.

lemon & papaya flatbread
Prepare the basic recipe, replacing the dried cranberries with
an equal quantity of dried chopped papaya.

ice cream pizza with brownie base

see base recipe page 265

chocolate ice cream pizza
Prepare the basic recipe, replacing the vanilla ice cream with an equal quantity of chocolate ice cream.

ice cream pizza with marscapone topping
Prepare the basic recipe, replacing the whipped cream topping with an equal quantity of marscapone.

rocky road ice cream pizza
Prepare the basic recipe, adding 25 g (1 oz) chopped walnuts to the brownie mixture once the flour has been incorporated. Replace the vanilla ice cream with an equal quantity of rocky road ice cream. Replace the assorted sweets with 25 g (1 oz) chopped walnuts.

ice cream pizza with butterscotch sauce
Prepare the basic recipe, drizzling 75 ml (5 tbsp) prepared butterscotch sauce over the layer of ice cream before adding the whipped cream and sweets.

variations

chocolate chip cookie base pizza

see base recipe page 266

butterscotch chip cookie base
Prepare the basic recipe, replacing the chocolate chips with an equal quantity of crushed butterscotch.

double chocolate cookie base pizza
Prepare the basic recipe, using a mixture of white and dark chocolate chips.

peanut brittle cookie crust pizza
Prepare the basic recipe, replacing the chocolate chips with an equal quantity of crushed peanut brittle.

toffee chip cookie base pizza
Prepare the basic recipe, replacing the chocolate chips with an equal quantity of crushed toffee.

variations

raspberry almond pizza

see base recipe page 269

raspberry almond pizza with chocolate drizzle
Prepare the basic recipe, drizzling each pizza with 60 ml (4 tbsp) melted chocolate chips after the raspberries and sliced almonds have been arranged.

raspberry almond pizza with cookie base
Prepare the basic recipe, replacing the basic thin pizza base with 400 g (14 oz) prepared sweet biscuit dough. Roll cookie dough out to form two 30-cm (12-in) pizzas, using scraps of dough from first pizza to help make the second. Adjust the oven temperature if necessary.

blackberry almond pizza
Prepare the basic recipe, replacing the seedless raspberry jam with an equal quantity of seedless blackberry jam and the fresh raspberries with an equal quantity of fresh blackberries.

variations

fig, ricotta & honey pizza

see base recipe page 270

fig, ricotta & honey pizza with thyme
Prepare the basic recipe, sprinkling 1.25 ml (¼ tsp) dried thyme over
the layer of ricotta cheese.

fig, ricotta & maple syrup pizza
Prepare the basic recipe, replacing the honey with an equal quantity
of maple syrup.

fig, mascarpone & honey pizza
Prepare the basic recipe, replacing the ricotta cheese with an equal
quantity of mascarpone.

strawberry, ricotta & balsamic pizza
Prepare the basic recipe, replacing the fig slices with 50 g (2 oz) hulled
strawberries per pizza. Replace the honey with 10 ml (2 tsp) balsamic
vinegar per pizza.

index

Almond
apple cranberry pizza with almonds 273
blackberry almond pizza 280
raspberry almond pizza 269
raspberry almond pizza with chocolate drizzle 280
raspberry almond pizza with cookie base 280
anchovy
Neapolitan pizza with 141
anchovy, olive & tomato pizza 56
caramelized onion, anchovy & olive pizza 45
pizza margherita with anchovies 50
tapenade pizza with anchovies & red pepper 82
Ancient Greeks 6
apple
apple cranberry pizza 254
apple cranberry pizza with almonds 273
apple cranberry pizza with coconut 273
apple raisin pizza 273
bliny with grated apple 166
cardamom apple pizza 273
flatbread, sweet fried with apple compote 276
apricots, dried
barley bread with 169
arepas 233
blue corn flour 247
coconut 247
stuffed with scrambled egg 247
wholemeal 247
artichoke
artichoke heart & ricotta calzones 87
artichoke heart calzones with basil 104
artichoke heart calzones with four cheeses 104
artichoke heart calzones with garlic and pepper 104
artichoke heart calzones with pancetta 104
artichoke heart calzones with white clams 104

fresh tomato pizza with marinated artichoke hearts 84
pesto & artichoke heart pizza 78
pizza margherita with artichoke hearts 50
Parisian pizza with 134
Asiago
broccoli, asiago & garlic calzones 108
broccoli, asiago & pine nut calzones 95
spinach, asiago & pine nut calzones 108
asparagus
prawn & asparagus panzerotti 107
vegetarian pizza with asparagus 52
aubergine
pesto & roasted aubergine pizza 78
steak & aubergine pizza 55
autumn pizza 80

Bacon
cheddar & bacon stuffed pizza 101
cheddar & bacon stuffed pizza with herb base 112
cheddar, bacon & pea stuffed pizza 112
cheddar, bacon & tomato stuffed pizza 112
pizza with the works & bacon 53
spinach, bacon & chèvre pizza 76
balsamic vinegar
balsamic garden vegetable pizza 77
chèvre, rocket & pear with balsamic vinegar pizza 85
strawberry, ricotta & balsamic pizza 281
bammy bread 234
beet & cassava 248
carrot & cassava 248
potato 248
sweet potato 248
bannock 227
with blueberries 244
cinnamon 244
with cranberries 244
with raisins 244
barbari 204
with feta 217
with nigella seeds 217

with oats 217
with raisins 217
with sunflower seeds 217
barley bread
barley & oat bread 169
barley & quinoa bread 169
barley & spelt bread 169
barley breakfast bread 159
barley injera 194
with butter & jam 169
with dried apricots 169
hono with barley 163
basil
artichoke heart calzones with basil 104
fontina & basil piadine 98
fontina, broccoli & basil piadine 110
fontina, ham & basil piadine 110
fontina, tomato & basil piadine 110
mozzarella & basil pesto stromboli 109
Neapolitan pizza with 141
prawn & basil panzerotti 107
beef
pizza with the works & roast beef 53
beef, corned
montreal pizza with 137
beef, ground
gorditas 230
rustic ricotta & ground beef pizza 106
Turkish pizza with spiced ground beef 136
beetroot
beetroot & cassava bammy bread 248
bianca pizza 67
four-cheese pizza bianca 81
pizza bianca with black olives 81
pizza bianca with rosemary 81
pizza bianca with sesame base 81
pizza bianca with prawns 81
bliny 152
buckwheat 166
with grated apple 166
with grated potato 166
with raisins 166
wholemeal 166

blueberry
bannock with blueberries 244
lemon & blueberry flatbread 277
blueberry jam
pan fry bread with wild blueberry jam 245
bocconcini
tapenade pizza with 82
fresh tomato pizza with 84
pizza margherita 35
Boursin
caramelized onion & Boursin pizza 56
garden vegetable pizza 60
sausage, mushroom & boursin calzones 113
bread
barley breakfast 159, 169
corn and cheese 249
jamaican bammy 234
navajo 228
pan fry 228, 245
broccoli
broccoli & mushroom calzones 108
broccoli & sun-dried tomato calzones 108
broccoli, asiago & garlic calzones 108
broccoli, asiago & pine nut calzones 95
broccoli, parmesan & pine nut calzones 108
fontina, broccoli & basil piadine 110
Brooklyn gourmet pizza 120
meat lovers' 135
with ratatouille 135
salmon 135
sausage 135
vegetarian 135
butterscotch
butterscotch chip cookie base pizza 279
ice cream pizza with butterscotch sauce 278

Calzones
artichoke heart & ricotta 87
artichoke heart calzones with basil 104
artichoke heart calzones with four cheeses 104

artichoke heart calzones with garlic and pepper 104
artichoke heart calzones with white clams 104
basic base 18
broccoli & mushroom 108
broccoli & sun-dried tomato 108
broccoli, asiago & garlic 108
broccoli, asiago & pine nut 95
broccoli, parmesan & pine nut 108
crab & chives 111
crab & Italian parsley 99
crab & mussel 111
crab & sweet corn 111
crab & thai basil 111
sausage & mushroom 102
sausage, mushroom & boursin 113
sausage, mushroom & pepper 113
sausage, mushroom & sun-dried tomato 113
scallop & crab 111
prawn panzerotti 92
smoked tofu & mushroom 113
turkey pepperoni & mushroom 113
cardamom
cardamom & allspice flatbread 197
cardamom & cinnamon flatbread 197
cardamom apple pizza 273
cardamom chocolate flatbread 197
cardamom flatbread 187
cardamom walnut flatbread 197
poppy seed flatbread with 221
cassava
beetroot & cassava bammy bread 248
carrot & cassava bammy bread 248
cayenne pepper
papadum with 190
cornbread with 249
cheddar
cheddar & bacon stuffed pizza 101
cheddar & bacon stuffed pizza with herb base 112
cheddar, bacon & pea stuffed pizza 112
cheddar, bacon & tomato stuffed pizza 112
oatcakes with aged cheddar 168

cheese
artichoke heart calzones with four cheeses 104
cheese ciabatta 162
cheese focaccia 161
cheese lefse 164
classic cheese pizza 31
corn & cheese bread 249
flatbread, crisp rye with 165
four-cheese deep-dish pizza 140
four-cheese pizza bianca 81
garlic & cheese hearth bread 220
garlic & olive oil pizza with 54
pancetta & cheese pizza 48
Parma ham & cheese pizza 48
pepperoni & cheese pizza 48
pizza with the works & cheese base 53
prosciutto & cheese pizza 48
salami & cheese pizza 48
three-cheese stromboli 109
chèvre
chèvre, rocket & field mushroom pizza 85
chèvre, rocket & olive pizza 85
chèvre, rocket & pear pizza 74
chèvre, rocket & pear with balsamic vinegar pizza 85
chèvre, rocket, pear & prosciutto pizza 85
chèvre, rocket, pear & walnut pizza 85
crab & chèvre pizza 57
pizza margherita with chèvre 50
spinach, bacon & chèvre pizza 76
tapenade pizza 69
vegetarian pizza with roasted root vegetables, pesto & chèvre 52
wild mushrooms with parsley & chèvre on basic base 79
Chicago deep-dish
basic pizza base 22
chicago deep-dish pizza 130
chicken
bbq chicken & fontina pizza 49
gorditas with 246
grilled chicken & fontina pizza 32
grilled chicken & pesto pizza 49
grilled chicken & sun-dried tomato pizza 49

grilled chicken with crispy onion pizza 49
jerk chicken with cheese pizza 49
louisiana pizza 127
sope with 250
chickpea flatbread 183
with ground pomegranate seeds 195
with mint 195
with saffron 195
with smoked paprika 195
chocolate
cardamom chocolate flatbread 197
chocolate chip cookie base pizza 266
chocolate chip flatbread 275
chocolate ginger pizza 272
chocolate hazelnut pizza 272
chocolate ice cream pizza 278
chocolate orange pizza 272
chocolate pizza 253
chocolate raspberry pizza 272
double chocolate cookie base pizza 279
flatbread, sweet fried with chocolate hazelnut spread 276
raspberry almond pizza with chocolate drizzle 280
chutney
oatcakes with onion chutney 168
parathi with 192
sausage & chutney pizza 51
ciabatta 146
cheese 162
thyme 162
with flax seeds 162
with sea salt 162
with smoked paprika 162
cinnamon
cardamom & cinnamon flatbread 197
cinnamon bannock 244
cinnamon flatbread 275
flatbread, sweet fried with cinnamon sugar 276
clam
artichoke heart calzones with white clams 104
clam pizza with roasted garlic 57
prawn & clam panzerotti 107
seafood pizza 46

coconut
apple cranberry pizza with coconut 273
arepas 247
cookie base pizza
butterscotch chip 279
chocolate chip 266
double chocolate 279
peanut butter chip 279
raspberry almond pizza with cookie base 280
toffee chip 279
coriander seeds
sangak with 216
corn
corn & cheese bread 249
corn injera 194
corn patty (sope) 238
louisiana cheese and corn pizza 138
cornbread 237
with cayenne pepper 249
with dill 249
with sweet red pepper 249
corn flour chapatti 189
cougette
steak & courgette pizza 55
crab
crab & chèvre pizza 57
crab & chives calzones 111
crab & Italian parsley calzones 99
crab & mussel calzones 111
crab & sweet corn calzones 111
crab & thai basil calzones 111
scallop & crab calzones 111
seafood deep-dish pizza 140
prawn & crab panzerotti 107
cranberry
apple cranberry pizza 254
apple cranberry pizza with almonds 273
apple cranberry pizza with coconut 273
bannock with cranberries 244
cranberry vanilla cranberry flatbread 275
lemon & cranberry flatbread 262
cream cheese
crab & Italian parsley calzones 99
smoked salmon & caper pizza 70

crème fraiche
    wild mushroom & crème fraiche
        pizza 79

base
    basic calzone 18
    basic chicago deep-dish pizza 22
    basic double pizza 19
    basic gluten-free pizza 24
    basic Neapolitan pizza 20
    basic pan pizza 16
    basic thin pizza 17
    basic Turkish pizza 21
    basic wholemeal thin pizza 23
    rye (montreal pizza) 137

Deep-dish pizza
    chicago 130
    four-cheese 140
    sausage 140
    spinach 140
    vegetable 140
dosa 180
    with ghee 193
    with omelet 193
    with onions 193
    semolina 193

Egg
    creamy spinach & egg pizza 76
    parathi with 192
egg, scrambled
    arepas stuffed with 247
equipment 8
escargots
    Parisian pizza with 134
escarole
    spinach, escarole & swiss chard
        pizza 76

Farls 156
fennel seeds
    flatbread, crisp rye with 165

feta
    barbari with 217
    Greek pizza 116
    manakish with 214
    spinach & feta pizza 59
    spinach, feta & olive pizza 76

spinach, feta & sun-dried tomato
    pizza 76
tapenade pizza with feta & cherry
    tomatoes 82
vegetarian pizza with 52
fig
    fig, mascarpone & honey pizza 281
    fig, ricotta & honey pizza 270
    fig, ricotta & honey pizza with
        thyme 281
    fig, ricotta & maple syrup pizza 281
    hawaiian pizza with figs 132
    spicy moroccan flatbread with 196
flatbread, cardamom 187
    with allspice 197
    with cinnamon 197
    with chocolate 197
    with walnut 197
flatbread, chickpea 183
    with ground pomegranate seeds 195
    with mint 195
    with saffron 195
    with smoked paprika 195
flatbread, crisp rye 151
    with cheese 165
    with fennel seeds 165
    with flax seeds 165
    with herring 165
    with sesame seeds 165
flatbread, lemon & cranberry 262
    with blueberry 277
    with cherry 277
    with currant 277
    with papaya 277
flatbread, poppy seed 212
    with cardamom 221
    with celery 221
    with cumin 221
    with garlic 221
    with smoked paprika 221
flatbread, spicy moroccan with olives
    184
    with currants 196
    with figs 196
    with peppers 196
    with sun-dried tomatoes 196
flatbread, sweet fried 261
    with apple compote 276
    with sweet pecans 276
    with chocolate hazelnut spread 276

with cinnamon sugar 276
flatbread, vanilla 258
    with carob 275
    with chocolate chip 275
    with cinnamon 275
    with cranberry 275
fontina
    artichoke heart calzones with four
        cheeses 104
    bbq chicken & fontina pizza 49
    fontina & basil piadine 98
    fontina & spinach piadine with
        nutmeg 110
    fontina, broccoli & basil piadine 110
    fontina, ham & basil piadine 110
    fontina, tomato & basil piadine 110
    four-cheese pizza bianca 81
    grilled chicken & fontina pizza 32
    prawn panzerotti 92
    three-cheese stromboli 109
fougasse
    with chili peppers 160
    classic 143
    with rosemary 160
    with sun-dried tomatoes 160
    with walnuts 160
    wholemeal 160
four seasons pizza 66

Garlic
    artichoke heart calzones with garlic
        and pepper 104
    broccoli, asiago & garlic calzones
        108
    clam pizza with roasted garlic 57
    garlic & cheese hearth bread 220
    garlic & olive oil pizza 43
    garlic & olive oil pizza with cheese
        54
    garlic & olive oil pizza with flat-leaf
        parsley 54
    garlic & olive oil pizza with
        kalamata olives 54
    garlic & olive oil pizza with sesame
        seed base 54
    garlic & olive oil pizza with prawn
        54
    garlic & parsley hearth bread 220
    garlic & pink peppercorn hearth
        bread 220

garlic & poppy seed flatbread 221
garlic & rosmary hearth bread 220
garlic & thyme hearth bread 220
garlic hearth bread 211
garlic naan 188
garlic pitta chips 218
lefse with 164
mozzarella & garlic stromboli 109
papadum with 190
rustic pancetta & mortadella pizza
    with garlic & peppers 105
ghee
    chapatti with 189
    dosa with 193
    naan with 188
gluten-free
    basic gluten-free pizza base 24
    gluten-free base 24
    pizza margherita on gluten-free
        pizza base 50
    sausage & pepper pizza on gluten-
        free pizza base 51
gorditas 230
    with chicken 246
    with green salsa 246
    stuffed with prickly pear 246
    wholemeal 246
Greek pizza 116
    on gluten-free base 133
    with kalamata olives 133
    with lamb 133
    with marinated tofu 133
    with tzatziki 133
Gruyère, smoked
    steak & mushroom pizza 44
    vegetarian pizza with 52
guacamole
    sope with 250

Halvah
    matzoh with 214
ham
    fontina, ham & basil piadine 110
    hawaiian pizza 115
    mozzarella & ham stromboli 96
havarti
    havarti & Parma ham stuffed
        pizza 112
Hawaiian pizza 115
    with figs 132

with grapes 132
with Parma ham 132
with prosciutto 132
on wholemeal base 132
herring
flatbread, crisp rye with 165
honey
fig, mascarpone & honey pizza 281
fig, ricotta & honey pizza 270
fig, ricotta & honey pizza with
thyme 281
matzoh with 214
sri lankan coconut roti with 191
hono 148
with barley 163
with caraway seeds 163
with celery seeds 163
with cheese 163
with sunflower seeds 163

Ice cream pizza
with butterscotch sauce 278
with brownie base 265
chocolate 278
with marshmallow topping 278
rocky road 278
injera 181
barley 194
corn 194
rice 194
wheat 194

Jamaican bammy bread 234

Lamb
Greek pizza with 133
Turkish pizza 123
lavash 208
with cumin seeds 219
with ground sumac 219
with poppy seeds 219
with sunflower seeds 219
with toasted sesame seeds 219
lemon
lemon & blueberry flatbread 277
lemon & cherry flatbread 277
lemon & cranberry flatbread 262
lemon & currant flatbread 277
lemon & papaya flatbread 277

lobster
Louisiana pizza with 138
Louisiana pizza 127
with buttom mushrooms 138
with cheese and corn 138
with lobster 138
with okra 138

Mackerel
caramelized onion & smoked
mackerel pizza 56
smoked mackerel pizza 83
manakish 200
with black olives 215
with feta 215
with fresh mint leaves 215
with pickled turnip 215
with tomato 215
maple syrup
fig, ricotta & maple syrup pizza 281
pan fry bread with 245
margherita
pizza margherita 35
pizza margherita on gluten-free
pizza base 50
pizza margherita with anchovies 50
pizza margherita with artichoke
hearts 50
pizza margherita with chèvre 50
pizza margherita with olives 50
Queen Margherita 35
masa harina
arepas 233
gorditas 230
masa harina tortilla chips 243
masa harina tortillas 224
masa harina tortillas with chili
pepper 243
masa harina tortillas with mixed
peppercorns 243
pupusa 241
sope 238
mascarpone
fig, mascarpone & honey pizza 281
mascarpone streusel pizza 274
matzoh 199
with halvah 214
with honey 214
with poppy seeds 214
with sesame seeds 214

with tahini 214
merguez sausage
rustic ricotta & merguez pizza 106
Mexican pizza 128
with coriander 139
with green salsa 139
with hot peppers 139
on tortilla 139
millet chapatti 189
Monterey Jack
cheddar & bacon stuffed pizza 101
corn & cheese bread 249
gorditas 230
jerk chicken with cheese pizza 49
monterey jack & three-pepper
piadine 110
seafood deep-dish pizza 140
tex-mex pizza 139
Montreal pizza 124
with corned beef 137
with hot peppers 137
with mustard 137
with pastrami 137
with rye base 137
mortadella
rustic pancetta & mortadella pizza
88
rustic pancetta & mortadella pizza
with garlic & peppers 105
rustic Parma ham & mortadella
pizza 105
rustic prosciutto & mortadella pizza
105
mozzarella
mozzarella & basil pesto stromboli 109
mozzarella & garlic stromboli 109
mozzarella & ham stromboli 96
mozzarella & pepperoni stromboli
109
mozzarella & tomato stromboli 109
mushroom
broccoli & mushroom calzones 108
caramelized onion & mushroom
pizza 56
chèvre, rocket & field mushroom
pizza 85
louisiana pizza with button
mushrooms 138
sausage & mushroom calzones 102

sausage pizza with mushroom
ragout 51
sausage, mushroom & boursin
calzones 113
sausage, mushroom & pepper
calzones 113
sausage, mushroom & sun-dried
tomato calzones 113
smoked tofu & mushroom calzones
113
steak & mushroom pizza 44
steak & mushroom pizza with herb
base 55
steak & mushroom pizza with
onions 55
steak & mushroom pizza with
raclette cheese 55
tapenade pizza with shiitake
mushrooms 82
turkey pepperoni & mushroom
calzones 113
mushroom, wild
wild mushroom & crème fraiche
pizza 79
wild mushroom & sage pizza 79
wild mushroom & sausage pizza 79
wild mushroom & tapenade pizza 79
wild mushrooms on wholemeal base
pizza 64
wild mushrooms with parsley &
chèvre on basic base 79

Naan 171
with cumin 188
garlic 188
with ghee 188
with nigella seeds 188
Navajo bread 228
Neapolitan pizza 131
with anchovies 141
basic pizza base 20
with fresh basil 141
with herb base 141
with ricotta 141
with sardines 141

Oats
barbari with 217
barley & oat bread 169

oatcakes 156
  with aged cheddar 168
  with bran 168
  with marmite 168
  with onion chutney 168
  with strawberry jam 168
olive oil
  garlic & olive oil pizza 43
  garlic & olive oil pizza with cheese 54
  garlic & olive oil pizza with flat-leaf parsley 54
  garlic & olive oil pizza with kalamata olives 54
  garlic & olive oil pizza with sesame seed base 54
  garlic & olive oil pizza with prawn 54
olives
  anchovy, olive & tomato pizza 56
  caramelised onion, anchovy & olive pizza 45
  chèvre, rocket & olive pizza 85
  garlic & olive oil pizza with kalamata 54
  Greek pizza with kalamata 133
  manakish with black 214
  pizza bianca with black 81
  pizza margherita with 50
  sope with green 250
  spicy Moroccan flatbread with 184
  spinach, feta & olive pizza 76
onion
  caramelized onion & boursin pizza 56
  caramelized onion & gorgonzola pizza 56
  caramelized onion & mushroom pizza 56
  caramelized onion & smoked mackerel pizza 56
  caramelized onion, anchovy & olive pizza 45
  dosa with 193
  focaccia with caramelized onions 161
  grilled chicken with crispy onion pizza 49
  sausage & pepper pizza with three onions 51

smoked salmon & red onion pizza 83
  steak & mushroom pizza with onions 55

Pan fry bread 228
  with fresh tomato salsa 245
  with maple syrup 245
  with sugar & lemon juice 245
  with wild blueberry jam 245
pancetta
  artichoke heart calzones with 104
  pancetta & cheese pizza 48
  provolone & pancetta stuffed pizza 112
  rustic pancetta & mortadella pizza 88
  rustic pancetta & mortadella pizza with garlic & peppers 105
panzerotti
  prawn 92
  prawn & asparagus 107
  prawn & basil 107
  prawn & clam 107
  prawn & crab 107
  prawn & scallop 107
papadum 175
  with cayenne 190
  with cumin 190
  with garlic 190
  with pink peppercorns 190
paprika, smoked
  chickpea flatbread with 195
  ciabatta with 162
  poppy seed flatbread with 221
parathi 178
  with chutney 192
  with egg 192
  with pomegranate seeds 192
  with potatoes 192
Parisian pizza
  with rocket 134
  with brie 134
  with camembert 134
  with escargots 134
  with grape tomatoes 134
Parma ham
  havarti & Parma ham stuffed pizza 112
  hawaiian pizza with Parma ham 132

Parma ham & cheese pizza 48
  rustic Parma ham & mortadella pizza 105
pastrami
  montreal pizza with 137
peanut butter
  peanut butter chip cookie base pizza 279
pear
  chèvre, rocket & pear pizza 74
  chèvre, rocket & pear with balsamic vinegar pizza 85
  chèvre, rocket, pear & prosciutto pizza 85
  chèvre, rocket, pear & walnut pizza 85
pepper
  artichoke heart calzones with garlic and 104
  cornbread with 249
  mexican pizza with hot peppers 139
  monterey jack & three-pepper piadine 110
  montreal pizza with hot peppers 137
  pesto & roasted red pepper pizza 78
  pizza with the works & three peppers 53
  rustic pancetta & mortadella pizza with garlic & peppers 105
  sausage & pepper pizza 36
  sausage & pepper pizza on gluten-free pizza base 51
  sausage & pepper pizza with three onions 51
  sausage, mushroom & pepper calzones 113
  spicy moroccan flatbread with 196
  tapenade pizza with anchovies & red 82
peppercorns
  garlic & pink peppercorn hearth bread 220
  masa harina tortillas with mixed 243
  papadum with pink 190
pepperoni
  classic pan pizza with the works 40
  fresh tomato pizza with pepperoni 84
  mexican pizza 128

mozzarella & pepperoni stromboli 109
  pepperoni & cheese pizza 48
pesto 26
  four seasons pizza 66
  garden vegetable pizza with 77
  grilled chicken & pesto pizza 49
  mozzarella & basil pesto stromboli 109
  pesto & artichoke heart pizza 78
  pesto & roasted aubergine pizza 78
  pesto & roasted red pepper pizza 78
  pesto & sun-dried tomato pizza 78
  pesto pizza 63
  pesto pizza with sesame base 78
  seafood deep-dish pizza 140
  vegetarian pizza with roasted root vegetables, pesto & chèvre 52
piadine
  fontina & basil 98
  fontina & spinach piadine with nutmeg 110
  fontina, broccoli & basil 110
  fontina, ham & basil 110
  fontina, tomato & basil 110
  monterey jack & three-pepper 110
pine nut
  broccoli, asiago & pine nut calzones 95
  broccoli, parmesan & pine nut calzones 108
  spinach, asiago & pine nut calzones 108
pineapple
  hawaiian pizza 115
pitta 207
  garlic pitta chips 218
  with hummus 218
  with pomegranate & mint dip 218
  with tzatziki 218
  wholemeal 218
pizza sauce, basic 25
pomegranate seeds
  chickpea flatbread with ground 195
  parathi with 192
  pitta with pomegranate & mint 218
poppy seeds
  lavash with 219
  matzoh with 214

poppy seed flatbread 212
sangak with 216
pork
sope with 250
Turkish pizza with 136
potato
bliny with grated 166
parathi with 192
potato bammy bread 248
prawn
garlic & olive oil pizza with 54
Parisian pizza 119
pizza bianca with 81
seafood pizza 46
prawn & asparagus panzerotti 107
prawn & basil panzerotti 107
prawn & clam panzerotti 107
prawn & crab panzerotti 107
prawn & scallop panzerotti 107
prawn panzerotti 92
prosciutto
chèvre, rocket, pear & prosciutto
pizza 85
hawaiian pizza with 132
prosciutto & cheese pizza 48
rustic prosciutto & mortadella pizza
105
provolone
provolone & pancetta stuffed pizza
112
rustic pancetta & mortadella pizza
88
rustic ricotta & salami pizza 91
three-cheese stromboli 109
pupusa 241
filled with cheese and herbs 251
fillled with chicharron 251
filled with green salsa 251
rice pupusa 251

Quinoa
barley & quinoa bread 169
rustic ricotta & quinoa pizza 106

Raisins
apple raisin pizza 273
bannock with 244
barbari with 217
bliny with 166

raspberry
chocolate raspberry pizza 272
raspberry almond pizza 269
raspberry almond pizza with
chocolate drizzle 280
raspberry almond pizza with cookie
base 280
raspberry jam
sri lankan coconut roti with 191
ratatouille 29
Brooklyn gourmet pizza with 135
rice
injera 194
pupusa 251
ricotta
artichoke heart & ricotta calzones 87
artichoke heart calzones with
pancetta 104
broccoli, asiago & pine nut calzones
95
cheddar & bacon stuffed pizza 101
fig, ricotta & honey pizza 270
fig, ricotta & honey pizza with
thyme 281
fig, ricotta & maple syrup pizza 281
four seasons pizza 66
louisiana pizza 127
Neapolitan pizza with 141
pizza bianca 67
ricotta streusel pizza 274
rustic pancetta & mortadella pizza
88
rustic ricotta & ground beef pizza
106
rustic ricotta & merguez pizza 106
rustic ricotta & quinoa pizza 106
rustic ricotta & roast vegetable pizza
106
rustic ricotta & salami pizza 91
rustic ricotta & spinach pizza 106
spinach & feta pizza 59
strawberry, ricotta & balsamic pizza
281
rocket
chèvre, rocket & field mushroom
pizza 85
chèvre, rocket & olive pizza 85
chèvre, rocket & pear pizza 74
chèvre, rocket & pear with balsamic
vinegar pizza 85

chèvre, rocket, pear & prosciutto
pizza 85
chèvre, rocket, pear & walnut pizza
85
Parisian pizza with 134
rocky road ice cream pizza 278
Romano
four-cheese pizza bianca 81
roti
sri lankan coconut 176
sri lankan coconut roti with
raspberry jam 191

Salami
rustic ricotta & salami pizza 91
salami & cheese pizza 48
salmon
Brooklyn gourmet salmon pizza 135
smoked salmon & caper pizza on
wholemeal base 83
smoked salmon & fresh tomato
pizza 83
smoked salmon & red onion pizza
83
smoked salmon & caper pizza 70
salsa, green
gorditas with 246
Mexican pizza with 139
pupusa filled with 251
salsa, tomato
pan fry bread with fresh tomato
salsa 245
sardines
Neapolitan pizza with 141
sauce 25
basic pizza 25
sausage pizza 28
sauerkraut
sausage & sauerkraut pizza 51
sausage
basic sausage sauce 28
Brooklyn gourmet sausage pizza 135
pizza with the works & sausage 53
rustic Italian sausage pizza 105
rustic pancetta & mortadella pizza
88
sausage & chutney pizza 51
sausage & mushroom calzones 102
sausage & pepper pizza 36
sausage & pepper pizza on gluten-

free pizza base 51
sausage & pepper pizza with three
onions 51
sausage & sauerkraut pizza 51
sausage deep-dish pizza 140
sausage pizza sauce 28
sausage pizza with mushroom
ragout 51
sausage, mushroom & boursin
calzones 113
sausage, mushroom & pepper
calzones 113
sausage, mushroom & sun-dried
tomato calzones 113
wild mushroom & sausage pizza 79
sausage, spicy
mexican pizza 128
seafood
seafood deep-dish pizza 140
seafood pizza 46
seafood pizza with tomatoes 57
smoked meat
montreal pizza 124
sope 238
with chicken 250
with chili pepper 250
with green olives 250
with guacamole 250
with shredded pork 250
spinach
creamy spinach & egg pizza 76
fontina & spinach piadine with
nutmeg 110
rustic ricotta & spinach pizza 106
spinach & feta pizza 59
spinach, asiago & pine nut calzones
108
spinach, bacon & chèvre pizza 76
spinach deep-dish pizza 140
spinach, escarole & swiss chard pizza
76
spinach, feta & olive pizza 76
spinach, feta & sun-dried tomato
pizza 76
squid
seafood pizza 46
Sri Lankan coconut roti 176
with banana 191
with honey 191

with raspberry jam 191
with treacle 191
steak
steak & aubergine pizza 55
steak & mushroom pizza 44
steak & mushroom pizza with herb base 55
steak & mushroom pizza with onions 55
steak & mushroom pizza with raclette cheese 55
steak & zucchini pizza 55
strawberry
strawberry, ricotta & balsamic pizza 281
strawberry jam, oatcakes with 168
streusel pizza 257
mascarpone streusel pizza 274
ricotta streusel pizza 274
streusel pizza with mixed berries 274
streusel pizza with raspberries 274
stromboli
mozzarella & basil pesto 109
mozzarella & garlic 109
mozzarella & ham 96
mozzarella & pepperoni 109
mozzarella & tomato 109
three-cheese 109
stuffed pizza
cheddar & bacon with herb base 112
cheddar, bacon & pea 112
cheddar, bacon & tomato 112
havarti & Parma ham 112
provolone & pancetta 112

Tahini
matzoh with 214
tapenade 27
tapenade pizza 69
tapenade pizza with anchovies & red pepper 82
tapenade pizza with bocconcini 82
tapenade pizza with roasted veggies 82
tapenade pizza with shiitake mushrooms 82
wild mushroom & tapenade pizza 79
Tex-Mex pizza 139
tofu
Greek pizza with 133

smoked tofu & mushroom calzones 113
tomato
anchovy, olive & tomato pizza 56
cheddar, bacon & tomato stuffed pizza 112
fontina, tomato & basil piadine 110
fresh tomato pizza 73
fresh tomato pizza with bocconcini 84
fresh tomato pizza with marinated artichoke hearts 84
fresh tomato pizza with oregano 84
fresh tomato pizza with pepperoni 84
fresh tomato pizza with saint-agur 84
manakish with 214
mozzarella & tomato stromboli 109
pan fry bread with fresh tomato salsa 245
Parisian pizza with grape tomatoes 134
seafood pizza with tomatoes 57
smoked salmon & fresh tomato pizza 83
tapenade pizza with feta & cherry tomatoes 82
tomato, sun-dried
broccoli & sun-dried tomato calzones 108
fougasse with 160
grilled chicken & sun-dried tomato pizza 49
pesto & sun-dried tomato pizza 78
sausage, mushroom & sun-dried tomato calzones 113
spicy Moroccan flatbread with 196
spinach, feta & sun-dried tomato pizza 76
tortillas 242, 223
blue corn 243
herb 242
masa harina 224
masa harina tortilla chips 243
masa harina tortillas with chilli pepper 243
masa harina tortillas with mixed peppercorns 243
mexican pizza on tortilla 139

spicy tortilla chips 242
sun-dried tomato 242
wheat 223
wheat tortilla chips 242
wholemeal 242
turkey pepperoni
turkey pepperoni & mushroom calzones 113
turkey, spiced ground
Turkish pizza with 136
Turkish
basic pizza base 21
Turkish pizza 123
with crumbled feta 136
with spiced crumbled seitan 136
with spiced ground beef 136
with spiced ground pork 136
with spiced ground turkey 136

Vanilla flatbread 258
vegetable
balsamic garden vegetable pizza 77
deep-dish pizza 140
focaccia with summer vegetables 161
garden vegetable pizza 60
garden vegetable pizza with cauliflower 77
garden vegetable pizza with herb base 77
garden vegetable pizza with pesto 77
rustic ricotta & roast vegetable pizza 106
spring vegetable pizza 77
tapenade pizza with roasted veggies 82
vegetarian
Brooklyn gourmet vegetarian pizza 135
vegetarian pizza 29
vegetarian pizza with asparagus 52
vegetarian pizza with feta 52
vegetarian pizza with leeks 52
vegetarian pizza with roasted root vegetables, pesto & chèvre 52
vegetarian pizza with smoked Gruyère 52

Walnut
cardamom walnut flatbread 197
chèvre, rocket, pear & walnut pizza 85
fougasse with 160
wheat
injera 194
tortillas 223
wholemeal
arepas 247
basic thin pizza base 23
bliny 166
chapatti 189
gorditas 246
pitta 218
smoked salmon & caper pizza on wholemeal base 83
tortillas 242
wild mushrooms on wholemeal base pizza 64
winter pizza 80
works, the
classic pan pizza with 40
pizza with the works & bacon 53
pizza with the works & cheese base 53
pizza with the works & roast beef 53
pizza with the works & sausage 53
pizza with the works & three peppers 53